Photo Bomb

Take Your Family Photos From Ordinary to Outstanding

Glenn Nielsen

Photo Bomb

Take Your Family Photos From Ordinary to Outstanding

Pics In The Glenn
info@photobombbook.com

Edited by Charlene Jones
Cover Design by ShakeCreative

Library of Congress Control Number: 2015940350
ISBN: 978-1-4951-5149-1

Published by Pics In The Glenn
Picsintheglenn.com

Printed in the United States of America

Since going professional in 2009, I have studied with many of today's great artists and attended numerous workshops and seminars only to walk away wondering, "Will I ever get this?" Most instructors explain the technique of manual photography in ways as convoluted as the "Quantum Theory"! Thankfully, in his book, "The Photo Bomb", Glenn explains in detailed, understandable terms about the graphics of Professional Photography, how to adjust your camera to "manual", and how to use the camera's various functions to produce great images. This book is a must-read for the novice considering taking the next step in Professional Photography. Great job, Glenn!

Terri Daunic

Table of Contents

Part I: Cell Phone and Point and Shoot Cameras

Chapter 1

Photography is Important to You

The purpose of Photo Bomb is three fold. First, and perhaps the most important to you, the author would like to help you become a better photographer providing the secrets and giving you the tools to enhance your cell phone photography to as good as it gets. Secondly, for those who have a digital camera to take you beyond fully automatic settings. Experience the control you gain by using the semi- automatic or manual capabilities and the difference that makes in your photography. Thirdly, the author would like to encourage you to think of photographers as you think of other professionals in your daily life. They are not someone you need to consult every day, but there are clearly times when hiring a professional photographer is appropriate.

Find a photographer with whom you can form a relationship and then nourish that relationship until it is as important to you as your doctor. In the spirit of collaboration, create a relationship with your photographer. You don't expect your dentist to brush your teeth every night, however, you don't try to straighten your own teeth or fill that cavity. You rely on the professional to take care of that. You don't see the dentist more than once or twice a year, but you have created a lifetime relationship despite this fact. The same is true of every professional with whom you have a business relationship.

When it comes to photography, often you think that you don't need the professional. The cameras are very well constructed and are fully capable of creating great images on full automatic. There are very sophisticated point and shoot cameras. The cell phone is small, convenient, and always with us. It is the number one camera in the world. It has become the standard against which we evaluate an image. For everyday events the cell phone camera is an excellent companion to document your life and the lives of your family and friends. You are able to instantly share your life, your events with hundreds or even thousands of people through social media. We have come to expect instant gratification. We want to share everything in our lives and participate in the lives of all our friends. It is not important that

Julie's face is yellow. It is important that you have captured Julie's gorgeous laugh. You have captured the magic of the moment.

Special events command more attention to detail. You think about getting better pictures, but you have a friend or husband who has a camera and can take the pictures for you. Again most images will be taken with your cell phone and the cell phones of other guests. Images will be posted before the last guest arrives. You tag everyone there so that they see the images also. The publicity is phenomenal and real time. Those who were unable to attend your event can participate through social media. The chances you would need a printed image are low. You might save the images to your computer. However, unless you have a newsletter or blog for which you are going to write something about your event that image will probably never leave your phone. Even if you have a newsletter or blog, chances are only a few of the images might be included as digital images.

Life events usually warrant selecting a professional photographer to document the moment. It is expected that you have a professional photographer at your wedding, perhaps a videographer also. However, does that mean that guests with cell phones and Uncle Bob with his professional camera are not completely documenting the big day? Absolutely not. This is the moment that collaboration becomes most important. In order for the bride to get the images for which she has paid the professional, it is important that everyone else respect his/her space. A good photographer will work with the guests to ensure that they also get great images of the event. The guests must also work with the photographer to ensure he/she can create the images that bring the bride to tears of joy when she sees them. Would you allow your friends to bring their own wrench and work on the engine of your brand new BMW 7-series while the mechanic was trying to tune the engine? A ridiculous question, right?

Wouldn't it be wonderful if you could establish a personal relationship with your photographer so that he could help you improve your skills with the camera so that you were getting better images for your everyday events and you would be perfectly comfortable having him as part of your family for the special and life events for which the value of the professional photograph is unquestionable. The goal of Photo Bomb would be to encourage you to seek a photographer with whom you have a long-time relationship, to build that bond between your family and your photographer. The final result will be a collaboration to achieve the best record of your family's highlights.

Five Quick Takeaways

Photo Bomb would like to help you improve your photographic images. Here are five quick tips that can help you maximize your cell phone's ability to get a great photo. There will be a more in depth discussion in later chapters why it is to your advantage to know your cell phone's strengths and limitations.

1. Stabilize your phone. Cell phone cameras aren't able to take in as much light as full function cameras, it becomes even more important to give it as much support and stability as possible. Hold the camera phone with both hands and brace your upper arms against your body when you shoot. If there is a table or wall against which you can brace your cell phone use it to provide additional stability.

2. Clean your lens. It may seem obvious or silly, but give your lens a wipe down before you start snapping photos with your phone. While most people are pretty good about keeping their fingers away from larger camera lenses, it's not as easily done with smartphones. You probably don't pay much attention to your smartphone lens while you are talking or texting with someone. If your lens is dirty, nothing else will help.

3. Pay attention to the light. Look for light with direction and color. This type of light happens naturally at just before sunrise and at sunset. Window light is also a good bet because it has direction and is often diffused, so it's not too harsh on your subjects. With a smartphone, you do not have the ability to make creative adjustments to focal length and aperture settings, so light and composition become more important for creating visual interest.

4. Don't use digital zoom. Unless you've got one of the best camera phones on the market, you are most likely working with digital zoom (as opposed to optical zoom). This means that you are using a smaller part of the sensor image from your smartphone. If you need to get closer to a subject, just step closer to them. If you can't, you can always crop the picture later on, which is all digital zoom really does.

5. Look for something special. Maybe it's people relaxing in the park. Maybe it's a quarrel on the street. Always be alert to a photo opportunity, and use these moments to practice. After all, the best camera is the one you have with you.

Chapter 2
Why Write Photo Bomb?

I grew up on a farm in southwestern Utah. There wasn't much discretionary money. The money we had was used to pay for food, shelter, and necessary farm expenses. Every day I worked side by side with my father. From him I learned the value of hard work, resourcefulness, and most importantly, the value of a man's word. Contracts were made on a handshake. We never worried about locking our doors. Our neighbors were our friends and we all worked together to get the tasks completed. The work day did not begin at 9:00 am and end at 5:00 pm. I remember many days when we were putting up the crops when the day would begin a 3:00 am because one had to wait for the dew to come in, but it was necessary to complete as much work as possible before that little bit of moisture was gone.

We were pretty isolated. Our nearest neighbor lived a quarter mile away. The nearest child my age lived nearly two miles away. I went to elementary school with about 15 children in my class. This was for two grades. The school house was about five miles away and gathered children from a radius of 12 miles.

There was always farm work to be done both before and after school. The one respite that I remember vividly was the Autumn day when my father took his 35mm film camera and we made a trip into the mountains to photograph the leaves turning color. I have an image etched in my memory of my sister and I, perhaps six and four years old, walking along the road in the mountains surrounded by brilliant yellow, red, and orange leaves on the trees. Somewhere that picture still exists. I believe that my sister has it.

As a photographer today, I strive to stop a moment in time for other families that holds the emotion of that image etched in my memory. I am writing this book because when that moment comes to you I want you to be able to capture it in an image that you can give to your children which will be etched in their memories forever.

My father gave me a Kodak™ box camera when I was a child. It was a film camera. I could take 12 pictures on a roll of film. There was nothing on or in the camera that I could adjust. I could look in the viewfinder, frame the image and then snap the picture. That was it. Then I would have to wait for about two weeks for the film to be sent to the lab for processing and the prints to be returned to me in the mail. I was so proud of those simple black and white images of the things around me. That was my introduction to photography.

After high school, I attended and graduated from the Air Force Academy and began to live my life long dream to be a fighter pilot. I graduated from Pilot Training at the top of my class and consequently was able to get my choice of available assignments of aircraft to fly. I chose the McDonald Douglas F-4 Phantom II. This was perhaps the most important decision of my life. After six months in Florida learning how to employ the fighter in its many roles, my first operational assignment was is Southeast Asia. I was assigned to Ubon Royal Thai Air Force Base in Thailand arriving there on the day after the North Vietnamese Army crossed the DMZ into South Vietnam in 1972.

Over the course of the next year I would fly 200 combat missions of which 100 were flown into North Vietnam. I was awarded the Distinguished Flying Cross seven times and the Air Medal 20 times. I grew up a lot in that year. I went from a naïve farm boy to a seasoned, confident, experienced fighter pilot. There was another event that also took place that year. I purchased my first Single Lens Reflex camera. It was a Minolta SRT 101. It was a very advanced camera. There was even a light meter built into the camera. You could point the camera at your subject, look through the view finder, find the object that looked like the hands of the clock, turn the shutter speed or aperture dials until the hand lined up with a circle. Then you took the picture and it was properly exposed - most of the time. I used this camera to take pictures of people and objects around me. During a brief period of Rest and Recreation (R&R) I went to Pattaya Beach in Thailand. I met an NFL football player who was touring with the USO. It was a unique situation. He wanted to do what we were doing and we wanted to do what he was doing, a mutual admiration society. At that time, Pattaya Beach was a fishing village, not the huge resort community that it is today. It was a well needed respite from the war and I had the opportunity to practice and improve my photographic skills.

I would take trips to the Buddhist Monasteries and Temples which are abundant in Thailand. They are absolutely gorgeous and provide unlimited photo opportunities. I would photograph the people and the poverty of the land. If the threat was not too great, I would even take the camera with me on a mission to photograph the airplanes in flight and the countryside below. I took hundreds maybe even thousands of slides and prints of my experiences. I read photo books and magazines to improve my skills. I would experiment with filters to create different effects.

After leaving the war, my next assignment was in Okinawa. I arrived there as the War in Southeast Asia was ending. President Nixon had just given Okinawa back to the Japanese people – it had been under American control since the end of the Second World War. We were a strategic force in Asia, able to deploy throughout the area to complete any mission necessary to protect our allies from the Communist threat of the Soviet Union and China. It was the middle of the cold war. While I was there President Nixon made his historic trip to China and the cold war began to thaw a little. Because of political agreements between the countries, we were asked to deploy to Taiwan as a defensive force to protect the Nationalist Chinese from the People's Republic of China forces. We would fly active air defense missions in the straits between the island of Formosa and Mainland China. For two and a half years I photographed the landscape and people of both Taiwan and Okinawa.

During this time I created a darkroom in my bathroom with developing trays spread across the floor of the bathtub and the enlarger sitting on the toilet. I was only able to work in the darkroom at night because that was the only time that I could block all of the white light from outside. It was a great time. I printed black and white images of F-4s on 24x24 paper and then wet mounted them onto a 20x20 wooden board. They were gorgeous. I also became the unofficial squadron photographer. I purchased a Mamiya RB67 medium format camera. I would use slide film to take portraits of the members of the squadron which I then mounted onto a large board which was lighted from behind. We were the only squadron that had such a fine display of the members of the unit. This was the peak of my early photographic career.

When I returned to Florida as an instructor pilot in the F-4, life and career began to get in the way of my photography work. I was still taking images, but the frequency of using the camera and the number of photographs taken began to decline. This trend continued when I was assigned to Germany for six years, first on an exchange tour with the German Air Force, and then for an assignment to NATO Headquarters in Heidelberg.

After leaving Germany my career was rounded out with an assignment at Goldsboro, NC as a Squadron Operations Officer and as Chief of Safety, again flying the F-4. My final assignment was to the staff of the Air War College in Montgomery, AL. There I had the opportunity to meet and to teach some of the most talented military leaders in the world. One of the officers went on to be the Chief of Staff of the French Air Force. Many others went on to be Generals and Admirals in the US armed forces. In 1992 I retired from the Air Force and moved to Tampa, Florida. My many years in the Air Force had reinforced the principles of discipline, dedication, and an attention to detail that carry forward into every relationship with my clients today. My word and a handshake bind me to complete any effort to which I commit myself.

After my mother died in 1999 my father expressed his desire to travel through the Panama Canal. Two years later we were able to bring that dream to fruition. My dad and I traveled to Los Angeles, CA where we boarded the Orient Cruise Lines™ M.V. Crown Odyssey ™for our journey. From there we traveled south stopping in Mexico and Costa Rica before turning west into the Panama Canal – The Pacific side of the canal is east of the Caribbean side of the canal. The journey was 16 days. Of course for such an important event I needed a camera to take pictures. I purchased a Nikon™ N80 film camera with which I proceeded to take many rolls of film. Our journey ended in Ft Lauderdale, FL and the fire that was my passion for photography had been kindled once again.

It was not until 2008 when my wife and I took a Viking River Cruise through China that the fire began to burn. After 16 days visiting some of the most ancient sites in the world, for which I had purchased my first digital camera, I had over 4000 images, most of which were good, a few of which were stunning. This was so exciting. Not only could I take great pictures, but I could see the results immediately. Of course I now needed software to be able to process the images. On the advice of many articles on the subject, I chose Lightroom®™ and Photoshop™. Then the very steep learning curve began, there was so much to learn in order to effectively use the programs. The more I learned, the more I realized I needed to know. After a year of struggling on my own, I discovered Meet Up and the photography groups within it. This was a Godsend. Now I could not only learn from others who had already gone down this path, but I could get great new ideas of how and why to take an image, how to see the whole image, not just the subject.

At about the same time, the opportunity arose for me to take an early retirement from my second profession, a data center manager for Verizon. I considered the options for six months before I decided that it was time for me to leave my corporate job of 16 years and work for myself instead. I took the leap into the cold water. I loved creating art with a camera; I was going to become a photographer. Unfortunately, the world was not waiting for me to make this decision and no one was beating down my door to get me to take pictures. I had a lot to learn. I worked on my technical skills for a year before it became obvious to me that my real weakness was lack of business acumen. So I began to work on business skills with the same passion I had for photography.

I learned that it was not practical to market everything that a photographer could provide to a client. What did I really want to photograph? What was it that really motivated me? After a lot of soul searching, I realized that it was people that made me feel good. If I could capture that smile, that glance between a mother and her daughter that held their love for each other, if I could capture that moment in their lives that would be etched in their memory forever - I would be successful.

In order to have any chance to see that instant, it would be necessary to develop a relationship with my clients. I realized how much I enjoy building those relationships. I do not thrive on selling fine art. I thrive on establishing a relationship with my clients so that I become a friend. I want them to be completely comfortable that my motivation is to give them the images that they want to proudly display on their living room wall for all of their friends to see. When they look at that image, I want them to remember how much fun it was, what a great experience they had when they took the image. In a perfect world, not only would the moment be etched into their memory forever, the experience would be something they would remember and talk about forever. It is the journey. The end product merely reminds one of how great the path to get there turned out to be.

Chapter 3
Welcome to the Revolution

There is a major revolution going on around us with which we are so involved, so close to the situation that often we don't even see the changes. They are incrementally small, but constant. The workers are becoming entrepreneurs instead of employees. The number of small businesses and small business owners is growing very rapidly both as an absolute number and as a percentage of the workforce. It is becoming more important to forge relationships with your competitors and clients. The relationship is more important than what you have to offer. Often, our clients are at the same time our competitors. We are expected to do more of the work ourselves. There are no more secretaries. Even executive assistants are rare today. Major advancements in technology have facilitated this process. Everyone has a computer, a laptop, a tablet, and certainly a smart phone. Each of these devises have simplified our ability to do our job effectively and released us from the need to rely on others for the products and services we need. "There's an app for that" has become the mantra for everyone. As we have moved away from specialization in the workplace to an expectation that everyone can do everything, we have also lost the precision of the specialist. Would anyone argue that the written words one sees in e-mails are as precise as the business letter fifty years ago?

The world of photography is not immune to these changes. On the contrary, everyone has a camera in their smart phone or their tablet. It is possible to take a photograph of an event and to post it on Facebook or Instagram immediately. Before the event has ended, the world has seen pictures of it and the people who participated and responded with a comment or two. There is an unspoken challenge to see who can get the images on social media first. This ability has had an immense impact on the quality of the images that are part of our everyday lives. We are so busy taking pictures that we do not see the beauty right in front of our eyes. How often have you been in the exact same place with someone else, both of you took an image of the scene, yet the images are very different. Sometimes the images are so different that you question if you were both at the same place.

In order to capture that special image you need to slow down and smell the roses. Look at the whole scene then look at tiny pieces of the scene. Is there a unique color combination? Is there a pattern that you never noticed before? Let yourself be open to the obvious that you have not previously seen. Take your time. If you move through a scene slowly you will have the opportunity to notice the little things that you're too busy to see as you rush from one point to another. You are searching for the gold and almost stumbling on it, yet you never see it. It is right there in front of you, yet you look past it. Look for them, the great pictures of the world are right in front of you. As an example to illustrate this point, there was a photographer in Dallas, TX who took a photograph at night of the tall buildings of downtown reflected in the water which lay before the photographer. The image is breathtaking. It made the photographer a lot of money licensing and selling that one image. Some of the other photographers were familiar with the exact spot where the image was taken. They knew that there was no body of water there. There was nothing but a parking lot. Cries of "You Photoshop'ed it" began to rise. The photographer quietly explained that the image was taken following a heavy thunder storm. The water in which the downtown scene was reflected was puddles of rain water in the parking lot. This photographer saw the scene and captured it. It could be said that the photographer was in the right place at the right time and that would be correct, but he saw the image probably because he was looking at everything in the scene. How many other photographers went past this exact spot at this time and never saw the extraordinary beauty before them. It was the same picture of downtown that they had seen a thousand times before, but it wasn't.

A mother is able to take hundreds of pictures of her family. The question Photo Bomb will pose is whether or not photography as an art is better off as a result of this informality. I would suggest that we have lowered our expectation of what constitutes a good photograph. At the same time, I would suggest that if the most uninitiated, untrained person were shown a cell phone image next to an image produced by a professional photographer that they would immediately recognize the difference. The purpose of Photo Bomb is to help the mom who is using the cell phone to take better images so she can record her most precious memories. Photo Bomb will raise your ability to "see" everything that makes the image have impact and make sure to include it and to "see" everything that detracts from the image or competes with the subject and diminish or eliminate it.

Photography is all about emotion and storytelling. The images that "tear our heart out" and bring us to tears have successfully captured both. As a photographer, you know that you have been successful when you show the images for the first time you see the tears well up in the mother's eyes or you hear the gasp followed by the WOW!!! An image with no emotion is documentation not art. Mothers are very good at capturing the emotion of their family because they are experiencing the same emotion as the people in the image. If they take enough photographs, they will have several they can proudly show their family and friends. The camera (cell phone) will take care of the technical details and get the exposure correct and be focused on something.

There are some things that the cell phone is not especially good at fixing. The most obvious is adjustments for the color temperature of the light which is dominant in the image. As humans, our eyes are capable of automatically correcting for the different temperatures of light. We don't notice that the bright sun at noon is a different color than the light from the living room lamp. We see both as correct. The camera is not so talented. That is why the image looks yellow when it is taken in the living room at night. You compensate for this by using the flash. That brings in a different set of issues because the intensity of the light from the flash diminishes very quickly the further away the subject is from the flash. So Susie may be properly exposed, but Johnny who is standing behind her is darker. The difference in light intensity is determined by how far away from the subject the flash is. The closer the camera (flash) is to the subject, the greater the light fall off. If you are taking the picture from across the room, you may not notice the difference and both Susie and Johnny are properly exposed. If you are standing three feet away from Susie, Johnny may be very poorly exposed. However, if you are standing across the room, the flash on your cell phone might not have enough power to properly illuminate either Susie or Johnny and the whole image is dark.

How do you resolve this dilemma? Compromise. By experimenting with the camera and flash, you should get comfortable with how far away to stand and get great exposure for Susie and acceptable exposure for Johnny at the same time. It also helps if you get Johnny to stand closer to Susie so that the effect of the light fall off is diminished. Photography is complex. With today's technology it is very easy to be an average photographer. Photo Bomb will provide you with the tips and suggestions to take you to the next level. You will enjoy clear explanations of the key points that take your image from interesting to WOW!!! If you're in a hurry and just want to learn how to take better pictures of your children, go to that section and follow the guidance. Get ready to improve your photographs.

Chapter 4
Why Do You Take Photographs?

If you are like most young people today, you learned at a very young age that you could improve your popularity by taking photos of your friends and then posting them on their social media. The rewards were instantly received and usually significant. Photography has become the method you use to maintain contact with those who are important to you. You use your cell phone to document the meetings and seminars that you attend. The organizers are very happy to get the publicity and encourage you to post event photography to all your social media outlets. Your friends all comment on what a great life you lead and how they envy you. Your cell phone quickly became a critical part of your wardrobe and went with you everywhere. Photography became routine, it was not something special, it was simply a part of your life. When you were young it was all about your friends, as you grow older and begin to create your own family, they become the center of your universe and the subject of most of your images.

When you think about why and when most mothers take pictures of their friends and family you could sort the times into three major groups: every day events, special events, and life impacting events. Almost all mothers are very comfortable using their cell phone to document everyday events and to get them posted to social media immediately so that everyone can enjoy the moment together. Mothers use social media to maintain contact with people who are important to them but may not live close enough for them to visit regularly. All their friends are present on social media. It is so cool for the mother to be able to live her friends' lives with them and to share her life with them.

Occasionally, something extraordinary is planned, a special event for someone special. This might include a birthday or anniversary party, a family reunion, a special vacation, or maybe even certain school activities like the prom or homecoming. Depending upon the relationship with her professional photographer, this might be a time that Mom would hire one to get that special photograph.

Life events are so special that one seeks a professional photographer to get high quality images worthy of the occasion. If Mom doesn't have an existing relationship with a photographer, she would probably ask her friends for a referral or seek advice from an internet search or one of the many online agencies like Angie's List™ or Yelp™. A wedding would immediately come to mind as a life event. You might also consider the birth of a child, or the purchase of your dream home as equally important.

You take tons of pictures when you go on vacation. Inside each of us is the desire to have that photograph of the Grand Canyon that no one else has been able to capture. Even though we have seen the travel brochures and explored the internet, the pure majesty of standing in front of that massive hole in the ground with all its beautiful colors and rock formations leaves us with a feeling that we have to capture. The camera is the medium that we use to capture it.

In the days of film, we would create a photo album of all our great travel photographs so that we could share our experiences with our friends and family members who were not able to enjoy our vacation with us. Today, more often than not, the album is in the cell phone and we show it to everyone. Even while we are on vacation we share the images with our friends through social media.

Chapter 5
Every Day Events: Improving Your Images

The easiest way to make a great improvement in your daily photography is to look at the scene, the lighting of the scene and try to reduce the contrast between the brightest and darkest areas within the scene. What does this mean? For example, if you are taking a picture of your children playing in the park at noon on a bright sunny day, the sun is very bright and any shadows that may exist are going to be very dark, relatively speaking. If you were to move the children into the shade and use something within the shade for your background, the contrast would be significantly reduced and the camera would stand a much greater chance to pick the proper exposure for the image. Because you are exposing the photograph for the illumination in which your subject is located the location of the camera is not important, it could be in the sun or in the shade.You could use the shadow of a building, if one exists, or you could use the shadow of the trees. The challenge with using trees to reduce the contrast is that you add another factor in that the trees do not stop all direct light unless the trees are very thick. Usually there will be spots where the direct sunlight falls through the trees and leaves a bright spot on the ground. You want to look for those spots and avoid having them fall on your children. If that is not possible, make sure the spots do not fall on your children's faces. If you can't avoid the sun spots find a different location.

The one situation that you want to avoid at all costs is having your children looking into a bright light like the sun or a reflector. Your children will squint to block the light and make it less painful. This is never a natural look by which you want to remember the event or your children. If you know you are going to be photographing in the bright sunlight and there is nothing you can do to avoid it, you can buy a collapsible reflector from a photography store for less than $50. You could then get someone to hold the reflector between the sun and your children thereby blocking the sun from your child's face. You want to be very conscious of the effect of the reflector. If you place the reflector too close to your children, you will create a shadow. Six to eight feet away should be sufficient. The light will spill around the reflector, but it will be much softer, meaning lower contrast. You can also use the reflector in a different way. You can position your children with the sun at their back or off at a slight angle. You can then get someone to hold the reflector near you, as the photographer, and reflect the sun's light back into your children's faces to reduce the contrast by filling the shadows with reflected light. If the reflection is too bright, move the center of the reflected light off of their faces to their bodies or to the side. You may have to really concentrate to see the reflected light until you get used to seeing it. There is a definite increase in the brightness of the shadow when the reflector is properly placed. This is a technique that you can use to reduce the contrast even when the sun is blocked by clouds. The reflection will be more difficult to see, but it is still there and it can still be used to lighten up the shadows on your children's faces. There are many different types of reflective material available. Each one has its own light characteristics. The most common reflector is silver. This will reflect a lot of light which may be a problem on a very bright day. You may need to direct the reflected light to the side of your subject yet close enough to get the effect of the lightening of the shadows on your subject's face. For working in bright sunlight a better solution might be to use a white reflector. White will give you a softer reflection with less contrast. This choice will also result in very little, if any, color shift. A gold reflector will add a yellow shift to the reflected light. This is a very pleasant effect if you are trying to “warm up” the photograph. It will give your subjects a slight tan. Many photographers like this effect because it makes the subjects look more alive. You can also find zebra reflectors. These are hybrids consisting of alternating stripes of either silver or gold and white. As you might guess, this will reduce the effect of the silver or gold reflector, but the effect is still there. To get the greatest flexibility with the least amount of equipment that you need to carry with you, I would recommend one of the five-in-one reflectors which are readily available and allow you to change the cover of the reflector. If you get a reflector, you will want to practice using it before your photography session. The ring which holds the fabric tight is elastic. When you take it out of the cloth bag in which it comes, it will spring from about a foot in diameter to about 3 feet in diameter. One challenge you will face is how to get it back into its bag. You might want to have someone demonstrate this technique, but grab one side of the reflector with one hand, turn your other hand upside down before you grab the other side then just turn your hand back over. This will cause the reflector to form a modified figure 8 and you can slide the loops over each other and slide into the bag. It sounds complicated, but if you practice a few times you can master the technique.

An alternative to the photographic reflector would be to buy a white shower curtain from any retail outlet. Cut the white cloth, not the plastic, into a square 3 to 4 feet on each side. Although not nearly as effective as the reflector, you could get someone to hold the cloth – you would probably need two people to do this – and use it as a reflector. The advantage here would be that you could fold up the cloth and put it in your purse and the white cloth would be better than nothing. If you are choosing this option, make sure that the shower curtain is pure white. Any color will add an unwanted tint to your photos. You could also purchase a white foam core sheet from your local office supply store. That would be rigid, enabling one person to effectively use it, but it would also be bulky.

Chapter 6
Special events: Raising The Bar

Birthdays and Anniversaries

Most birthdays and anniversaries pass with intimate celebrations and little fanfare. The cell phone is great for taking that image of everyone just before you leave the house for dinner, or at the restaurant, or whatever the destination might be. They are convenient, small, and always with you. The major advantage, and what makes them so popular, is that they can be used to post the images to social media immediately. Your friends and family members can see instantly where you are and what a great time you are having. Occasionally, there is a special birthday like “sweet sixteen” or “Lordy, Lordy Harry turned forty.” This may be the time to consider having a professional photographer as part of the festivities.

Family Reunions

The family reunion is the perfect time for you to collaborate with your professional photographer to ensure that all of the people who present at the reunion have wonderful memories of the event. There will be hundreds of photographs to be taken. Everyone will have their cell phone or digital camera to take their own pictures. These images will be enjoyed by everyone who sees them whether or not they were able to attend the reunion. However, there are also opportunities during the festivities to get the formal family group picture, the image that has everyone in it. Because of the size of the group and the limitation of the lenses that are used on the cameras today, there are a number of factors that must be considered in order to get that great family portrait. The fully automatic camera is able to solve some of those challenges, but the odds are that it will not solve all of them. The camera may think that one aspect is important while you consider something else more important. If you want to have control of all the variables you need to be familiar enough with your camera to make the settings yourself. Where are you going to take the image? The environment and the size of the group may dictate your location and you might have to do the best you can. If it's raining and you have to move indoors to take the picture are you going to have enough light to get the proper exposure? Are you going to be able to use a high enough aperture to get the depth of field that you need to get everyone in focus? Do you know how to determine the depth of focus to find out if you have a mission impossible? For most of your images, it really doesn't matter. As long as the person or event you were trying to photograph is recognizable you have been successful. However, the family reunion is something special. Especially if your gathering is large, you will be glad you had a professional photographer help you capture the emotion of the event. You want to have the images be beautiful and consequently be something very special to take home with the guests.

School activities

Are your children participating in extracurricular activities like sports or theater, or collecting groups? Can you imagine how excited your multi-sport son would be if he opened up a birthday present and it was a 6-ft poster of himself in a football uniform catching that touchdown pass that won the Homecoming game? But wait, there's more, what if that same poster had captured him standing at the plate just before he hit that home run. What if a picture of Prom Night and his car were also part of the poster? What if this montage was held together with lightning bolts? The resulting poster would be so awesome that he would put it up in his room immediately. Your daughter could have a painting made from the photograph of her with her pet parrot. You could have a poster made of various scenes from the school play. The only thing limiting what is possible to document the important moments in your children's lives is your imagination. All of what I have described is within the skill set of the modern professional photographer. It goes so far beyond what can be captured by the cell phone that it adds a completely new dimension. The images that you take with the cell phone are vital to showing everyday life. They allow you to share your proudest moments with your friends and relatives almost immediately. This is a dimension that was never possible for previous generations of teenagers. Facebook and Instagram have replaced the family scrapbook. The only thing that I would caution is that you consider the impact in your life if there are no permanent photographs of your family activities and technology has moved beyond social media and as a result you are no longer able to access the images that you posted for all the special events in your life. You don't think that it will happen, ask yourself when was the last time you used a floppy disk. Are you able to view the content of the floppy disks that you made and stored just five to ten years ago? When was the last time you used a CD? Technology is changing our world. It is important to have your own personal record of your life not dependent upon technology. A professional photographic print will last over 100 years. It is not impacted by changes in our surroundings or our machines.

Chapter 7
When a Cell Phone Really Isn't Good Enough

Marriage

A wedding is the one event for which most brides consider the services of a professional photographer as being essential. There are no "do overs." It has to be right the first time and the event is so important in the bride's life that she definitely wants to have photographs of the event which will last forever. For the best results, the bride should select a photographer who specializes in weddings. She should look at the photographer's website. Are there examples of families, pets, travel, etc., or are all of the images associated with a wedding? The more specialized the photographer, the more pleased the bride, and other interested parties such as her mother or the groom, will be with the results. The bride and groom should schedule a consultation with the photographer they are considering to hire. They need to spend the time to get to know the photographer. Is this someone with whom the bride is comfortable enough that she wants to spend the most important day of her life with them? The bride and groom should listen to what the photographer has to offer. Is it something that interests them? This aspect of the wedding should be a priority. The newlyweds will not always remember what they had for dinner at the reception, but they will always go back to their wedding album and relive the day, the excitement, the anticipation of what was to come, and the friends and family who shared the event with them.

It is important that the bride work with the photographer. If there are specific scenes she wants to create, or a special place where she wants the family group photographed, then that information should be discussed with the photographer well in advance of the big day. If this is to be an outdoor wedding, together the bride and the photographer should consider an inclement weather alternative, just in case. It is also important that the bride identify those guests who are critical to be included in the images from the event.

One thing that is often overlooked which will create drama at your wedding is how to deal with the guests who wish to take their own photographs of the wedding. This should definitely be discussed with the photographer ahead of time. An effective way to accomplish this is to include an insert with the wedding invitation requesting guests to be courteous to the professional photographer hired to record the events of the day. Request that the guests allow the photographer to be able to do what they have been paid to do. There will be an opportunity for the guests to get their own images after the photographer has completed their job. This simple note may prevent “Aunt Mable” from jumping into the aisle in front of the photographer just as he/she was about to capture the bride and her father coming down the aisle. If necessary, the bride could request that no cameras be brought to the wedding, although that might be a little harsh.

Newborn children

Following the wedding, the next most important event in most people’s lives is the birth of their children. For the mother there are many emotions as the pregnancy progresses. Her body begins to change shape, routines change, she is excited, yet anxious, about the actual birth. There is so much that is unknown. There are many friends and family members who give advice, and that helps, but it is still unknown exactly what will happen. The time passes quickly and it is easy to forget to schedule a photo session with your photographer. You may regret not having professional images of the beautiful glow that an expectant mother has about her.

Once the baby has been born there are immediate changes in Mom's life. She no longer gets to sleep through the night. There is someone constantly demanding attention. She must adjust her way of life. Within this turmoil she may wish to have images taken of her offspring. To capture the newborn's essence, a photography session should occur within the first two weeks after birth. If Mom has had maternity photographs taken, the photographer should already be on alert and be prepared to work with her to get this scheduled. The photographer will have suggestions for possible images. The mother should collaborate with the photographer to ensure that she gets the best possible images. This is a very intimate moment in time between mother and baby; Mom must be comfortable with the images that are being taken. Most importantly, everyone involved must think of the safety of the child. Make sure that someone is watching the baby at all times, never more than a foot away.

Ideally, the baby would have been fed just before the photo session, so it is necessary to consider feeding schedules when you decide on a time. Quality images will be more assured if the baby sleeps through the session. A warmer than normal room will help. If necessary, portable heaters could be placed near the studio area. A white noise generator, a ticking clock, or soft music will also help the baby sleep.

A mother will also want to capture her own images of the child's first days. She will probably use her cell phone for these images. She will have the opportunity to experience events that the professional photographer will not just because she is constantly with her baby. She should confidently take those pictures. Post them on Facebook and Instagram. Share them with her family and friends. In addition to her cell phone images she will have the photographs taken by the professional which together result in a great job of capturing the first days of the baby's life. Someday she may pass this along to her child when he is about to have children.

Another Life Event: A Promotion or A New job

Immediately following that promotion or being hired for the new job is an excellent time to consider getting a new professional portrait taken. This portrait represents you wherever you display it. This includes your social media as well as press releases and company literature. You want to portray yourself as the professional that you are.

A non-professional headshot tells the world that you do not care enough about your career to make the effort. If you will look at the photographs of the people on social media, people you may know with whom you may wish to create a contact, it will become obvious very quickly who has a professional portrait and who has a non-professional headshot, or even worse, a selfie. As you look at the images, ask yourself if you form a different opinion of the people without even knowing them just based on their photograph. Please do not underestimate the value of a professional portrait.

When you call a professional photographer to ask about a corporate portrait, the response you should expect is a series of questions to determine for what the image is to be used. There are many events that trigger the need for an executive portrait. Is it for a billboard, an ad piece, a book jacket, business cards, web bio page, trade publication, Autographed Black and White Glossies, or Comp cards? If the image is going to be used for an advertisement or for your web page you should consider what will be the best orientation of the verbiage and the image. Will the image be on the right or the left of the text? This might determine which direction to have your body facing. Also which direction you might want the light to come from. Is there a color scheme to the ad piece or the web site that needs to be considered? Do you have a Brand color that you want to emphasize? Should the background match a specific color scheme, or be neutral? Will you need only a head and shoulders image, or will a 3/4 length or full length be useful or needed in the future? Do you desire a posed image or should it be candid, photo journalistic, storytelling, action shots? Do you need a studio backdrop, or do you prefer an environmental scenario? Are you going to need the licensing to reproduce the image in print, or simply use it on the web? How soon do you need the image to be delivered? All of these questions lead to a more qualified determination of your investment in a professional quality executive portrait. Way too often, the caller assumes a head shot is just a head shot. Someone to push a button and email them a file - that's it. Save yourself the disappointment and find your satisfaction with an experienced professional, and let your executive portrait be far more than just "a head shot."

New home, Collectables, Documentation

Moving into a new home is an excellent reason to hire a professional photographer to take images of your home and furniture. This will provide irrefutable evidence of what you had should you need to make an insurance claim. It will also provide great pictures to post on social media to make sure all your friends and family see your new "digs." While you are at it, this might be a good time to photograph that coin or stamp collection you have, or all of your art work. Remember, "someday" is not a day of the week and if you ever need this documentation, it is most probably going to be too late to get it. That could cost you thousands of dollars in lost insurance settlements.

Chapter 8

If you want to take images of your friends and family that are truly excellent, what do you need to consider?

Improve Your Images

The family Portrait

The biggest challenge – getting yourself in the image. The only way to get yourself in the picture with a cell phone is to have someone else take the picture. So you hand your cell phone to someone, perhaps a total stranger, and ask them to take a picture of your family. Half of the time they don't even know what they need to do because they have a different phone and the buttons are different. You are completely at their mercy for composition, posing, lighting, and cropping. You will look at the image to see if it is good enough. If not you take another, or you ask someone else to take the photograph for you. The other option, which is becoming increasingly popular, is to take a selfie. From a photographer's view, the selfie is wrong in so many ways. The camera is too close, the images are distorted, the light is horrible, and you may or may not have an acceptable composition with all the proper people in the picture. The odds are that the clothing worn by the people in the image is not complimentary. Stripes and plaids, solids and patterns, every color you can imagine. Each of these factors detracts from the aesthetic impact of the image.

Composition

Whole books have been written just on the subject of composition. Photo Bomb is not going to add to that collection. There are, however, a few hints which can make a world of difference in the impact of your images. In photography the general rule is that symmetry is not a good thing. If the image is perfectly balanced it becomes less interesting. This is the basis for the often quoted rule of thirds. In its simplest form this can be described as imagining a tick-tack-toe grid over your image. The point of greatest impact is at the intersection of the lines. Add to that the fact that Americans read

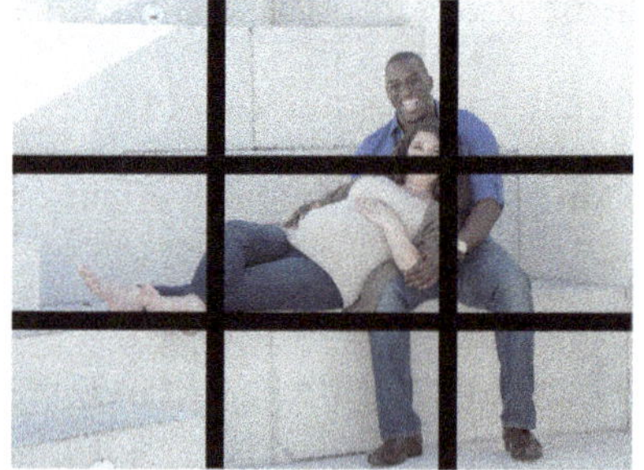

text from left to right and the left vertical line has slightly more impact than the right vertical line. One more consideration, we read from top to bottom. That means that the top horizontal line has slightly more impact than the lower horizontal line. As a result, if you want the subject to appear strong and powerful you would place it at the left upper intersection. If you want it to be less strong and powerful you would place it in the lower right intersection. Keep in mind that this is just one rule of composition. Other events or images within the photograph could be more impactful or cause these rules to be less significant. Most of all, keep in mind that these are rules and, once understood, rules are meant to be broken.

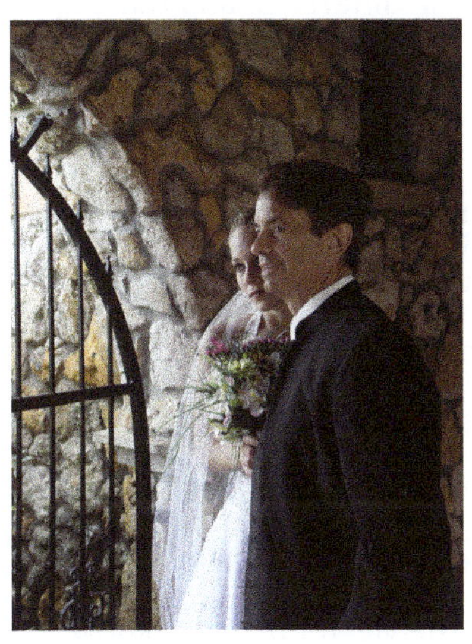

The next rule of composition that you should consider is what are called leading lines. Any time there is a continuous line within the image it becomes a leading line. It will lead your eye into the subject or away from the subject. This line does not have to be a pencil line. It could be a road, a fence, the horizon, or even the contrail from an overhead airliner. It does not have to be straight. Some of the best leading lines are curved. In this image the gate forms leading lines which draw your eye to the couple (the subject). The leading lines could be prominent or very subtle. As a general rule, this is not a part of the image you are composing in your mind and/or in the viewfinder of your camera. It may not immediately jump out at you. Often you will not even be aware of it until you look at your picture and you start to analyze it. However, if you were to look at a scene where the photographer saw the leading lines and used them effectively to guide the viewer's eyes and then look at the same scene where the photographer did not consider the leading lines and they were improperly placed, you would sense the difference and think that the image which considered the leading lines in the composition to be a much better photograph.

While discussing lines, it is important to keep lines which are supposed to be vertical straight up and down and lines which are supposed to be horizontal flat. Imagine if you took a picture of a lake or the ocean and the horizon slants. First of all the picture is out of balance. That is not a natural state of the world. The viewer's mind will immediately sense that imbalance and it will detract from the image even though the viewer may not know why. The same is true of buildings and rooms. Because of the distortion caused by the camera's lens, if you point the camera up to get the whole building into the picture, when you look at the image the building will appear to be falling backwards. Sometimes this is the effect that you are looking for and you are consciously breaking the rules. If you photograph a room and the camera lens is not perpendicular to the wall, the room will be distorted. There may not be a lot that you can do to prevent or to correct for this effect. You should be aware of the possibility and try to minimize the impact in your photograph.

You can add impact to your photographs by adding a natural frame. The most used example of this would be to include a tree branch which goes across the top of the image or perhaps a tree trunk down one side of the image. Anything which is not part of the subject can be used for this effect. It does not have to be in focus. In fact, it is more impactful if it is not in focus which would normally mean that the object which was creating the frame is either well in front

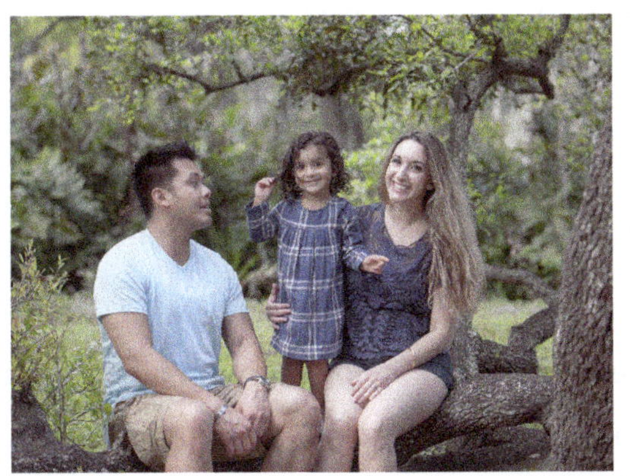

of the subject or well behind the subject. The subject of selective focus is described in greater detail in the Background section of this chapter. As you are composing the photograph look at the foreground and the background for objects that can enhance the image as well as for objects which can detract from the image. With a little concentrated practice you will become much more aware of what is not part of the image but is within the field of view of the camera and whether or not you want to emphasize or minimize the importance of those items.

Posing

Posing people is an art in and of itself. For most people posing would mean getting the tall people in the back and the short people in the front so you can see everyone's face. While it is important to be able to see everyone's face you should remember why you are taking the picture. Is there someone in the picture who is most important for the moment? This could be Mom and Dad if it is a family portrait. It could be the birthday boy if it were a birthday party. It could be the baby if you are photographing a new born child. Whoever the most important person might be, that is where you begin posing the group. Is this person going to be standing, sitting, kneeling, or laying down?

Have them get into the position you have envisioned in your mind for them. Then you need to determine who is next most important. That person should be placed very near your first subject, but not at the same level. Remember, in photography symmetry is boring. As a guideline, you would want the level of the eyes to be at the level of the mouth of the other person. Perhaps you would say that it is not possible to have everyone be exactly as tall as necessary to be able to line up mouths and eyes. You would be absolutely correct. However, think beyond the obvious. You could have people sitting and standing, or kneeling, or lying down. If legs are not in the picture, you could have a man stand with his legs apart. By doing this, you could get up to 6 inches of height change. You can also find something in the image area to stand on. Just make sure that the object can safely support the weight of the person standing on it. You could also make or buy blocks of varying heights so that you could stack them for additional height. You want to arrange people so that their heads form a check mark, or a W or an M or some combination to achieve the desired composition. Keep in mind that you do not want to have two adjacent people at the same height. That creates symmetry and that is less interesting.

As you begin joining people together keep in mind where your optical focus point is going to be. Normally you would envision a plane, a glass window, rising vertically from the ground through your key subject's head. You want everyone else to have their head as close to that plane as you possibly can. That will help keep everyone in focus. The camera focuses on one plane, one point. The further away from that point an object is placed, the less in focus it will be. This effect is also impacted by the distance the camera is from the subject and the amount that you as the photographer have zoomed into the image. For any camera and lens combination, the depth of field is the distance from the closest object which is acceptably sharp to the object furthest away which is still acceptably sharp. The depth of field is determined by a mathematical formula. For the iPhone 6 the camera has a fixed aperture of 2.2. If your subject is 10 feet away your depth of field is only three inches. At 20 feet the depth of field is nearly one foot. Most photographers, including professional photographers, do not feel the need to calculate that distance. It is not important that you know the numbers in this illustration. Suffice it to say that the closer the camera is to the subject, the shorter the depth of field. So if you are photographing a group which is large enough that there are three of four rows of people, you want to take the picture further away and not zoom into the picture. The other solution is to have the people in the back rows lean forward to get their heads closer to the focal plane you have selected, and within the depth of focus. This is one of the major weaknesses of the cell phone as compared to a digital camera.

Another rule of thumb, if you need to have the maximum possible depth of field, you should focus on a point which is one-third the distance from the closest point you want sharp to the farthest point you want sharp. This can be confusing so I will describe it in a different manner. On whatever subject you focus the lens, the area in acceptable focus will lie one-third in front of and two-thirds behind that subject. So you don't want to focus in the middle because your near objects may not be in focus if you do.

As you are posing your subjects you want to remember that a camera is trying to render a three dimensional object onto a two dimensional plane. Objects closer to the camera will appear larger than the same object further away from the camera. You can use this phenomenon to your advantage as you work to make everyone look their best. How often have you heard, "Please take off 20 pounds?" If you move the camera to a point which is slightly above your subject and then have the person lean forward slightly, you will have placed the upper part of their body slightly closer to the camera which will cause it to increase slightly in size while the lower part of the body will appear slightly smaller and you have gained the desired effect. If you try this, keep in mind that we are talking slight movements. You do not want to take the picture of the top of your subject's head. This would grossly distort the person and not be flattering. You also want to avoid having arms and/or legs pointing toward the camera. Have the person move their arms away from their waist. You want to be able to see light between the body and the arm. If you fail to create this visual effect, you will add 20 pounds to your subject because the arms will have the effect of adding to the mass of the body making it appear much larger. You can also use other objects, including people, to hide part of a person's body thus creating the illusion of them being more slender. You can use fences, trees, stair rails, chairs, tables, etc. You don't want to hide your subject completely, just enough of them to make them appear more slender.

Clothing

Coordinated clothing choices for a group photograph will have a major impact on the perceived quality of the picture, especially if the subject is a family or a work group. This is also an area where it is often difficult to get everyone to cooperate. People are very independent and have their own ideas of what constitutes good fashion. There is a considerable difference between trying to make a fashion statement, being the "coolest dresser," and getting an image that you are proud to show to your business colleagues. Color plays an important role in the way we dress and consequently the way we look. It is not necessary for everyone to dress in a white shirt and black slacks. It is very important that everyone dress tone in tone. That means all wearing soft pastels, or all earth tones, or cool tones. Here you will find some ideas for selecting groups of colors which complement each other.

Cool tones of denim and charcoal can be softened with a touch of soft grey and warmed up slightly with a little taupe or tan. Even a little brown or black fits in key for convenience.

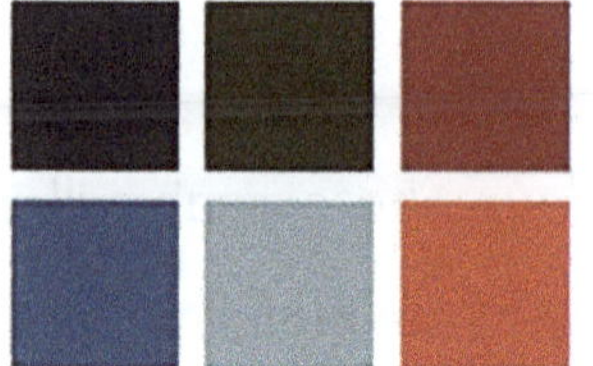

Burgundy, hunter and navy –or similar tones – make a great combo that is great for holiday times and all year too! Cranberry shades bring life without being an overpowering red.

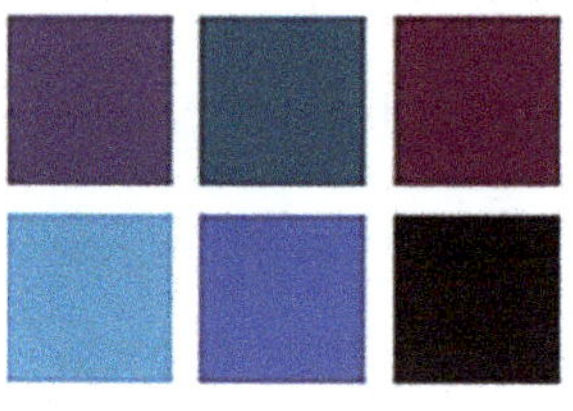

Rich jewel tones are easy to mix and match with black or even denim. All the vivid colors hold their own if they are medium to dark. NO LIGHT COLORS IN THIS COMBO

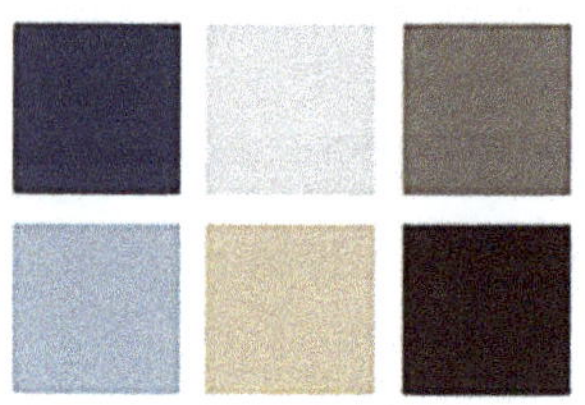

Browns, tans, khaki and beige, mixed with a bit of easy-going denim is a great palette for warm backgrounds and cool fall days!

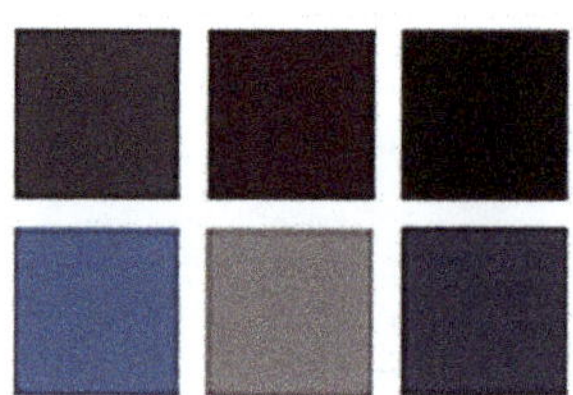

Black, charcoal, dark brown and taupe, even a burgundy-brown all coordinate well for any decor! Add some cool denim to mix it up or stick with all black bottoms.

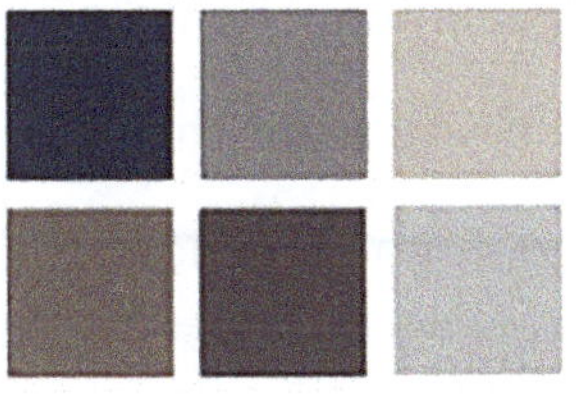

All the soft shades of sand, dry grass, and fields, taupe and camel! Every variation gives a little more dimension in such a classy way! Bottom it off with jeans or khaki!

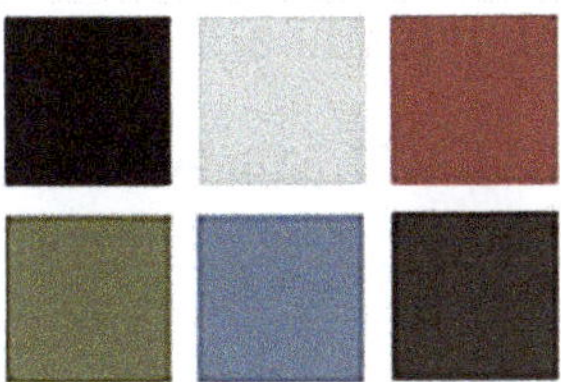

Rust and Hunter, sage and cream… always looks amazing with warm fall colors! And winter scarfs too!

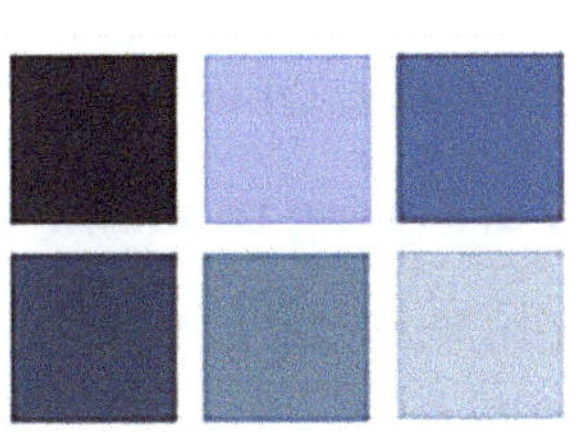

Denim is king… light or dark, chambray or stonewashed, dresses or shorts, everyone has jeans of some kind and they go together, no matter what the tone! Good Genes!

Time of day

Choosing the best time of the day for your picture can be challenging. Again, compromise may be the only solution. The best light from the sun is what is known as the "Blue Hour." This is the time from twilight to an hour after sunrise in the morning, and from an hour before sunset to twilight in the evening. The light at this time of day is very soft and low contrast. If you want the sunrise or sunset as an element of your image, it goes without saying that you must photograph within this time frame. There are some additional challenges which become an issue during this time. The first and most obvious is the sun itself. If you are shooting into the sun to capture the stunning sunset, you will need to get additional light onto your subjects. This can be accomplished with a reflector or with an additional light source such as a flash or strobe. Another option would be to use one or several flashlights to add light to your subjects' faces. Obviously if you shine a flashlight in someone's face, they are going to squint and that does not look good in the photograph. You can get around this issue by using a reflector or piece of large white paper or cloth. If you shine the flashlight into the reflector while holding it in front of the subjects you can add additional soft light to their face. Regardless how you add light to your scene, the biggest challenge that you will have is balancing the exposure needed for your supplemental light with the exposure needed for the natural environment. In order to get the most pleasing image, you would want the subjects' faces to be slightly brighter than the surrounding environment. Unfortunately, this is one situation where the point and shoot camera or cell phone will not correctly pick the exposure. Without making a correction as described, the camera will expose for the sunset and the people in the picture will be too dark, or it will expose for the people and the sunset will be way overexposed leaving no detail in the light parts of the image.

You can turn the situation around and have your subjects face into the sun, but you will now have issues with the distorted faces caused by squinting to reduce the brightness of the sun. You may also find that the brighter places on your subjects' faces will also be overexposed. With an iPhone you can reduce the overexposure of the highlights on the faces by tapping on the bright spots on the image before you take the picture. This should cause the cell phone to expose for the point you just touched which will reduce the overall exposure of the image and it will become darker. If you find that the faces are too dark, you can touch the screen at one of the darker spots and the camera will expose for that point and the image will become brighter. The best solution is if you can find something to block the direct sunlight from falling on your subjects so that you can reduce this super bright spots in the image.

There are times of the day other than sunrise and sunset when you will be photographing people. The absolute worst condition for the photographer is near midday when the sun is high in the sky. The shadows are sharp and clearly defined. If there are no clouds in the sky to soften the harsh rays from the sun, you need to find something else to help you. The first choice would be to find the shadow of a building or larger object which was large enough to get your subjects completely within the shadow. If you are able to find that shadow, you will lower the contrast of the scene and your camera will most probably be able to properly expose all objects in the photograph. A key consideration in this situation, you want your subject be the brightest thing in the image. This is important because eyes are drawn to the brightest point in the image. If you take the photograph with your subjects in the shadow but have the brightly lit environment as background, the brightest part of your image will be the background. Even if your subjects are properly exposed, your image will be less appealing because of the brightness surrounding them. You should always look at the whole situation before you take the picture. If there is no alternative, you only have midday available for the photo session, there is no shade, and you don't have a large enough reflector to block the sun, then you want to place your subject between you and the sun. That does not necessarily mean that the sun is directly behind them. As we already discussed, this would result in an overexposed background pulling our eyes away from the subject. You would also want to avoid having the sun directly right or left of you as you face your subject. That situation would result in half of your subject's face being overly dark, emphasized by the high contrast of the time of day. Look at the background. Are there trees which are darker that could be used to reduce the intensity of the background in your image? Be careful, however, to not have a tree growing out of your subject's head. Move the camera or move the subject so the tree is not directly behind your subject.

Lighting

We have discussed lighting several times already. It is important in every photograph you take. Light will make or break your image. You cannot always rely on your camera to get the proper exposure. The reality is that the camera will measure the light at the point where you are focused or it will measure the average light for the overall image area depending upon settings in the camera. There are formulas which consider the light in other parts of the image at a lesser value, but the most important area is where you focus. Logic tells us that this is the way it should be. Most of the time it is accurate and you get an acceptably exposed result. There are times when the camera will be fooled. Without getting too technical, the camera measures all light relative to the color grey. In any scene it will expose to get the majority of the image to a neutral grey light intensity. Most of the time, this is exactly what we want. However, if the majority of the colors in the image area are more white than grey, the camera will reduce the exposure to achieve the grey it seeks.

The result is that your white table cloth looks dirty, not sparkling clean as it really was. On the other end of the spectrum, if the majority of the colors are very dark or black, the camera will increase the exposure to compensate and the colors will look washed out. You may not notice this effect in the majority of your images, but think what the effect would be if you were taking a picture of your daughter, the bride, and her bridesmaids and they were all wearing very light colors. You are going to be very disappointed when you look at the photograph and you see a light grey wedding dress, not the bright white that it really was. Remember that with your iPhone you can tap on the dark part of your image and it will get lighter, you could tap on a dark spot to increase the exposure and get closer to the white you are looking for.

Not only does the intensity of the light impact your image, the temperature of the light also has a major impact on how your image looks. Have you ever taken a picture of your children playing in the living room at night and wondered why it was so yellow? That is because the camera is adjusting the rendering of the scene using the assumption that it is being illuminated by the sun, when in fact, it is being illuminated by household light bulbs. The scene really is that yellow, but our eyes compensate and everything looks normal to us. The camera records what it sees using the criteria which are built into it. In your own home you can correct for this effect by buying and using daylight light bulbs. They are readily available and produce light which is very close to daylight. It is also possible to get florescent light bulbs which are balanced for daylight where you might have florescent tube lighting.

The relative size of the illumination makes a big difference in the quality of the light. If you use a small light source like a flashlight to illuminate someone's face you will get harsh shadows and very hard light. If you shine that same flashlight into a reflector and let the light bounce back onto your subject, the light gets much softer and more pleasing. The size of the reflector is much greater than the size of the flashlight. We all know that the sun is very big, millions of times the size of the earth. However, it is a relatively small light source and creates harsh shadows and high contrast. This points out another quality of your light source, even if you use a large light source, if it is far away from your subject it becomes relatively smaller and harsher. That large light box that the photographer places four to six feet away from you that gives such a soft glow on your face would produce harsh shadows if it were moved farther away to light a larger area. If you want to have soft, even light across the entire scene you need to have a relatively large light source. This is why professional photographers have large light modifiers like umbrellas or light boxes on their studio lights.

The next quality that all light exhibits is a fall off of its intensity. You take a light and place it four feet from the subject and take a picture. Then you move the same light eight feet away from the subject doubling the distance the subject is from the light source. The picture you now take will only get one quarter of the light intensity which means that when you take the second picture the camera will need to increase exposure four times the original.

You may be asking yourself if you need to know this. The answer is no you do not, but you do need to understand that if you have two children in a room, one is close to the lamp and one is further away, the child who is further away will not be properly exposed. I'm sure that many of you have experienced this effect. Have you ever taken a photo of all your friends at a table in a darkly lit room using your camera's flash? Those people closest to the camera are overexposed and those farthest away from the camera are way underexposed. To get the best pictures, be aware of the distance your subject is from the illumination and try to get that distance as close to the same for everyone in the picture as is possible. Have people lean into the camera if they are farther away or arrange your friends in an arc so that they are near the same distance from the camera.

As you are composing your photograph think about what the light is doing to your subject. You can use light to get some great effects. Perhaps the most obvious effect would be the silhouette. There is very little detail, but a lot of mood and emotion can be generated. Have the light coming from behind your subject and don't use a flash to fill in the shadows in your subject's face. Depending on the intensity of the light surrounding your subject, you could have an image with no detail at all but a great outline of the body, or you could have an image where the subject is simply a little underexposed – only a good idea if you are doing it intentionally for a specific effect.

You can turn your subject 90 degrees so that you are taking a profile image. Again you could make a silhouette or you could properly illuminate the subject or you could be somewhere in between these two choices. When photographing more than one person, you need to be aware of each person's shadow and avoid letting it fall on another person or on the background. You can move the person closest to the light source back slightly and their shadow will fall behind the other person.

If you are using this technique you could also use the camera's quality of size distortion to place larger people further away from the camera which makes them appear to be smaller in the photograph. Size distortion will be discussed in detail under the perspective section which follows below

Background

Not paying attention to the background in your image is probably the most common mistake and the easiest to correct. As you are composing your image you are concentrating on the subject. Is it in focus, is it aligned properly for the composition you have chosen. Before you take that picture, stop, look at all four corners of the viewfinder. Make this a habit and you will avoid many bad shots. This takes discipline on your part as the photographer. All too often we are in such a hurry to get the photograph taken and move on. We think that our subject is impatient with us. We think that taking too long to compose and take the image means that we are unsure of ourselves or worse that we don't know what we are doing. So we rush it. Avoid that temptation. If you find that you are guilty of rushing the photo have someone work with you for a while. It does not have to be another photographer, although almost anyone today has some experience taking photographs. Use that other person as a crutch to get yourself to slow down. Make a checklist of the things that you want to consider in every image. For example you might list,

- Which rule of composition am I using? Have I composed correctly, or am I intentionally breaking the rule?
- Do I have something distracting in the background?
- Are there any bright spots in the image that I want to reduce or eliminate?
- Is there a tree or pole growing out of any of my subjects' heads?
- What am I going to focus on?

- Look at all four corners of the image. Is there anything that is detracting from your subject?

Have your assistant ask if you have completed each item in the checklist. If you do this it will quickly become routine and you will no longer need your assistant to question your steps in the checklist.

When selecting the background the first thing that you want to avoid is having the background being the brightest element of the picture. You can control this by selecting a different background, or use the following technique to make it darker, or to make your subject brighter. A simple neutral density or polarizing filter screwed onto the lens will darken the overall image. You could then use a flash or reflector to add additional light to your subject to get the proper exposure for them.

You could select a different time of day, perhaps early morning or late afternoon when the sun is not so bright. You could wait for a cloudy day when the sun's light is less intense. If you want that special shot, today, right now, may not be the time. You may have to come back. If there is only one opportunity, then you need to find a way to modify the background. (Worst case, if you have a tripod or some way to steady the camera where you know it will not move, you could take a picture of the background slightly underexposed, and then take a picture of your family properly exposed in front of the background. If you know someone with post processing software you could ask them to combine the two images to get the picture you had in your mind when you took it.) This process is an advanced technique that I do not recommend for images which are important to capture until you have practiced and succeeded. If the lighting is perpetually that challenging, it may be time to consider hiring a professional photographers who is familiar with light and the methods needed to harness it.

Next, you want to consider the focus of your image. Unless having the background sharp is critical to the composition of your image, you could move closer to your subject and have the background outside the depth of field so that it is not sharply in focus. Elements which are in focus are more important as we look at an image than the aspects which are not in focus. Look for leading lines or natural framing elements to bring attention to your subject. This technique was previously discussed in the Composition section. If there are leading lines in the picture area, make sure that they add to the overall composition and support your subject. They should not be too bright or sharp in focus unless at the same plane as your subject. Take your eyes to each corner of the image you are about to take and make sure that everything that is in the image is something you want in the image. Move if you must to remove unwanted distractions. You can also change the perspective, get lower, lie on the ground, get higher, stand on a ladder or box or anything stable. By changing the perspective away from eye level you change the image and its impact.

Foreground

Very rarely do we even think about the foreground of the image we are about to take. If there is something in front of the object we usually move it out of the way. However, if you want to add depth to your images, take a two dimensional rendering and make it appear to be three dimensional, then it is important to consider all three elements of the image, foreground, subject, and background. Adding a rock or plant in the foreground greatly enhances a landscape. I'm sure that you have all seen examples of this simple fact. It is not necessary for the foreground object to be in focus. If fact, if you are taking a picture of a vast landscape, you probably do not have the depth of field to get everything in focus from the front of the camera to the far horizon.

Depth of field and the factors that impact the area that can be in focus at one time have been discussed, as a reminder, the depth of focus is the distance from the nearest object which is in focus to the farthest object which is in focus. The three factors that impact depth of focus are the focal length of the lens being used, the aperture used to take the image and the distance that your primary object is from the camera. The longer the focal length of the lens (200mm vs 50mm), the greater the depth of field. The higher the aperture (f/16 vs f/2.8), the greater the depth of focus. The farther away from the main object the camera is, the greater the depth of focus. There are apps which can be used on the cell phone which will combine the lens, the aperture, and the distance to provide a depth of field as well as the distance to the nearest object in focus and the farthest object in focus.

You will recall that from the object on which you focus your camera, one-third of the depth of field will be in front of the object and two-thirds of the depth of field will be behind the object. So if you needed to take a photograph of the counter of a vegetable stand and you wanted the entire counter to be in focus, you would determine the lens to use and the aperture to set in order to get a depth of field equal to or greater than the length of the counter based on your distance from the center of the counter. You would then focus on a point that was one-third the distance from the front to the back of the counter and everything would be in focus. In order to make these adjustments you must have the ability to change the aperture settings in your camera or lens. Having a zoom lens allows you to adjust the focal length of the lens.

Perspective

As human beings, we view the world standing up, most of the time. As photographers, we take photographs standing with the camera at eye level. This gives nearly all photographs the same perspective. If you want to have an image that is different from everyone else's photograph change your position. Get down on the ground. Especially for pets and small children, get down to their level if you want to capture great pictures. I have seen an image of a snake where the camera was placed on the ground very near the snake to take the picture. I can assure you that the image was breathtaking. It looked completely different from the same image taken from normal standing height. A word of caution, if you are shooting up at a human, make sure that you are not looking up their nostrils. This is absolutely not a flattering view regardless how beautiful your subject may be. Have them lower the top of their head so that you are viewing the fullness of their face, or have them turn their head away from the camera.

Be very careful that an arm or leg is not pointing at the camera. You will get a very distorted view of your subject and the appendage will become the subject of your photograph regardless of what you intended when you began to pose the picture. While you are looking at the perspective, are you looking into the image or out of the image? Look for lines in your image. If you have a horizon, do not put it at the same level as your subject's head. Either stand on something sturdy to get above your subject so that the horizon is above it or kneel down so that the horizon is below your subject. Perspective does change the whole feeling of the image.

If the background makes the image symmetrical, move slightly to the left or right to get away from the symmetry. Moving a foot or two can create a completely different composition. If your intent is to create a symmetrical image, it is critical that the image is absolutely symmetrical. Every object on one side must be duplicated in the same position on the opposite side. If the image is not absolutely symmetrical it becomes very obvious and the image loses its appeal. That is why for the majority of your pictures, you are better off avoiding symmetry. The situation for which you will most often have to consider these points would be if you are photographing a church or a ceremony in a church. It is very common that the architecture of the vestibule is somewhat symmetric. Simply avoid standing in the middle of the aisle when you take your picture.

Chapter 9
Travel and Vacation Photographs

When you travel to someplace other than your home, whether it be for business or pleasure, you will want to capture the sights to show others and to keep the memory of the visit fresh in your mind. Especially if you are traveling for business, your photo opportunities may be very limited so you would want to maximize your opportunities. The internet is an outstanding source of information about your destination. Take a few minutes and do some research. Look at the pictures of the objects you would like to visit. Look for recommendations about the best time to photograph and suggestions about what to photograph. There are some basic things to think about. The best time to photograph a building or monument is going to be when the crowds are not so large. Look for a vantage point from which you get a new and refreshing view of the object. You do not want to have the same image that 10,000 other vacationers have taken.

It is a good idea to have something in the image which gives a hint to the size of the object you are photographing. A rock formation is interesting, however, a rock formation with a person standing in front of it or to the side of it presents a much different impression. Place something in the foreground to give depth to your photograph. It is amazing how much more interesting the Mittens in Monument Valley are with a sage brush bush in the foreground. Especially with landscapes, it is very important to show depth. Otherwise it is just a picture of mountains, nothing interesting.

Do not ignore the obvious. The room you are staying in can provide an excellent memory of your trip. Perhaps you counter by saying that there is nothing interesting about the standard side of the road motel in Americana. However, books have been published about Route 66 landmarks. In those books, exactly that type of motel room is prominently displayed. If you happen to be staying in the Berliner Hof in Berlin, Germany there is even more reason to remember your room. The odds are that you will not be back to this city or this room again. You have only one chance, don't discard it quickly. Take a picture of the view from your window. Today it may be dull and boring. Ten years from now it will be a wonderful memory.

Images of life on the street will probably become your most precious memories of your visit. If they do not object, photograph the people. Take pictures of the food, the drink, the local color. What is it that makes this place different than any other site on earth? That is what you want to capture. Look at perspective. What is in the foreground? Is it in focus? Should it be in focus? Are there natural frames to add emphasis to your subject? Are there vibrant colors in the clothing or in the architecture? Be sure to include your travel companions in your images. They will love the publicity having the photos posted to social media and it will add to your memories as you look back on the trip at some point in the future. Look beyond the obvious. Look for the untold story that is right in front of you. See the unseen.

Consider photographing your means of transportation. Train stations and airports for the most part are beautifully decorated and reflect the lifestyle of the cultures you are visiting. Subway stations often have beautiful frescos on the walls and columns with advertising again reflecting the local culture. Don't forget the busses. Nearly everyone immediately recognizes the red double decker buses of London. Depending upon the affluence of the lands you are visiting you may find the buses to be great photographic objects, but you would not be comfortable being on them for any length of time.

Churches and monuments are always great photographic subjects. Don't be afraid to get close and photograph the texture of the building. Capture the plates which describe the building and its historical significance. You will enjoy re-reading the information long after your vacation is over. Make sure that you are aware of and honor any restrictions which may be in place. Many churches do not allow tripods within the church. Often you can use a pillar or the back of a pew to steady your camera for exposures lasting more than 1/30 second. This is a situation where you may need to increase the ISO significantly in order to get an acceptable image.

Another great photographic opportunity can be found in local pubs and neighborhood gathering places. These as well as local restaurants will reflect the tastes of the local population. You may find stark facilities with no color at all, or you may find ornately carved wood with hundreds of colorful glasses and mugs everywhere. Either way the story told by the environment is well worth your effort to properly capture its beauty.

Chapter 10
Beginnings
Baby's First Year

Having a baby evokes so many emotions and changes to a mother's life yet only a few can be discussed here. This is not an owner's manual for your baby. This is a discussion of the life events that are associated with adding to your family. It is more a discussion of what you might want to do to have a permanent record of this miracle of life.

Maternity

An expectant mother has a glow about her. Despite being very uncomfortable with the changes that are occurring to her body, she knows that she is about to give new life to her family. The fear of the unknown , the anticipation of all the changes that will happen, the never ending questions about what to expect once the baby has been born all weigh constantly on her mind. Most of all, she is proud that she is participating in a miracle. It is important that this moment not pass so quickly that she only has memories of the wonder in which she has just participated. For centuries pregnant women were hidden from society. Today, maternity photography has become very popular. We proudly view images of our friends and family members as their bodies change. If you are going to photograph a pregnant woman, take the time to look at the image you are creating. Is it going to be a silhouette showing only the curves with a slight rim light to bring the body out away from the background? Maybe you would prefer a fully lit side profile clearly showing the "baby bump." Another option might be the mother and father using their hands to form a heart on the mother's belly. The key ingredient in this decision is the comfort level of the mother both with the photographer and with displaying her body for the camera. To capture the emotion of this moment is the dream of every maternity photographer. Not all succeed.

Newborn

This is the most critical phase of the first year of life. In order to capture the essence of the newborn, it is necessary to capture the images within the first 14 days following birth. After that changes begin to occur to the baby and the moment is lost forever. There are so many ways to take newborn photographs which range from a snapshot through the glass in the hospital to intimate professional images of mother, father, and baby. Again, the key to getting the great photograph is how comfortable the mother is with the photographer. There is a bond which is formed between the two which cements the emotions of the moment. There are so many things which can impact the success of the session. The room must be warm enough that the baby is comfortable. This is most probably in the high 70's or low 80's. Alternatively, space heaters could be placed near the baby to raise the temperature in the area immediately around the baby. It would also be wise to have a heating pad or an electric blanket to place under the baby. Be careful that the temperature is not set too high which could cause discomfort to the baby's tender skin. As a bit of common sense, if you are going to use a heating pad or an electric blanket, you would want to have the baby wearing a diaper. You do not want to risk getting liquid on the electric elements. A white noise generator will be helpful to calm the baby so he/she can and will sleep through most of the session. It is best to time the session so that it occurs immediately after the baby has been fed. Be prepared for the biological accident. It will happen. One way to be prepared is to have the baby wearing its diaper. However, the most beautiful images are of the baby in its natural state. This is how you really capture the emotions of the moment. You may want to consider placing a plastic sheet on the floor or underneath the blankets upon which you will lay the baby. It is advisable to have a sufficient supply of baby wipes. You also want to have hand sanitizer and use it often, especially whenever you are handling the baby.

Safety is critical. Never lay the baby down where there is any possibility that it could fall off of the prop. If you are using anything other than the crib, make sure that someone is constantly watching the baby to prevent any unexpected movements that could be dangerous. This goes without saying, but if you are handling the baby, be gentle and make sure that the baby's head is properly supported at all times. Patience is a virtue that you definitely want to exploit while photographing the newborn. There will be times when you will need to just hold your hand on the baby to provide that comfort until the baby goes back to sleep. Any props that you use must be clean and soft. Think carefully in advance how you plan to provide the light to illuminate the scene to get the correct exposure. You could use flash or strobes or you could use constant light. As is discussed in other areas of Photo Bomb each of these light sources have their own strengths and weaknesses. The advantage of continuous light is that the baby can move around without necessitating moving the light or adjusting the intensity. For each image, you can measure the exposure just before you take the picture and correct for any changes caused by the baby moving. The disadvantage is that the light is not as bright as strobes or flash so that you will need to increase the camera's sensitivity to light (ISO) in order to get the shutter speed high enough that the movements of the baby will not cause the image to be blurred. Throughout the photo session your primary thought should be that you do not want to be responsible for any injuries minor or major to the infant. Patience! Think about the consequences before you move. Make sure you have backup props, especially blankets or bedding, so that you can continue to capture the baby's expressions after the biological incident occurs. If you have a cold and cannot reschedule the session, use a medical mask to cover your face so you don't spread any germs to the baby. It would be good to have a conversation with the mother when you are scheduling the photo session to make sure that the baby is not allergic to anything that you might inadvertently bring to the location.

There are many unique attributes of the newborn that you would want to look for and photograph. Generally, the newborn will be content to sleep. Look for that grin that will come while the baby is sleeping. Newborns love skin to skin cuddling. If the mother and father are comfortable with the situation, look for and pose the baby in the mother's or father's arms held close to their face. The baby will love the skin to skin contact and the parents will love the photograph. If the baby wakes during the session, often you can gently touch the baby in order to get it to go back to sleep. If the baby cries this is normally a request for food or comfort. It is best to not ignore this request from the newborn.

The newborn will clench his fists which will make it difficult to get an image of the hands, but the feet make an excellent subject for an image. Don't be afraid to get close up images. Use the depth of field to keep certain body parts in focus and others blurred. Generally, you would want to have enough detail to know what was in the background, but not enough detail that it detracts from the image.

Three-month session

By the baby's third month they will start playing with their hands. The hands will be open and the baby will make sweeping motions and a chopping motion with the arms. The baby will hold and shake a rattle which can make an excellent photo opportunity. The baby will roll from their back to their side and can sit up and will play sitting semi-upright better than lying on the back. If there is a mobile in the crib, the baby will swipe at the hanging objects. The infant will play with their hands at times will appear to be flapping wings. They will suck on fingers and fists. Your subject may be able to stand for brief periods of time with help. Generally speaking look for props which will allow the baby to sit up such as pillows. You may want to try handing the baby a ball or a soft toy for them to play with. This is still the time that the baby wants to have physical contact with their parents. Images of mother and baby, father and baby, and siblings with baby are all precious. If there are siblings, you would definitely want to include them in some of the photos. You should discuss with the mother if the baby has recently started a new behavior. If yes, this would be a perfect opportunity for you to capture this behavior. The baby's movements will not be excessive, most probably they will be limited to the immediate area where the child is set down. It would be prudent to get some basic photographs and then be patient to capture the special moments.

Six-month session

By the time the baby has reached six months they will be able to sit briefly without help using arms for balance and for breaking falls. The child may slump forward as they are sitting. They are able to sit in a highchair. The baby will reflect moods by sound and body language. Expect shouts, belly laughs, clapping arms, grunts, growls, and even a droopy face. They mimic facial gestures, like to play with blocks and to bang toys. Set up your lights so there is a six foot by six foot area that has good lighting everywhere within it, then place the baby on the floor with their toys within the lighted area and wait for the magic to happen. You may get lucky and catch the infant trying to figure out how to pick up a third block when there is already a block in each hand. The expressions are without limit. The child will be able to roll in either direction so make sure that you have spotters for safety. Try to anticipate when something new is going to happen. The baby will be able to stand while holding on to a piece of furniture. This would be a good opportunity to bring some props into the photo session, a baby-sized chair or settee would provide something to hang onto as well as someplace to sit. At some point the baby may even begin to cry. Do not be afraid to take images of the baby crying. You may just capture an unforgettable image.

Nine-month session

By the time the baby has reached nine months they will be crawling. This could make your photo session more interesting. If you have a very active subject, you will need to have a larger area with the correct lighting if you are using studio strobes or constant lighting. If there is sufficient light in the room to allow you to increase the camera's ISO to get sharp images then you may find it easier to not use strobes. If you need to be able to move your lights as the baby moves, you may want to consider having a flash on a pole with a remote trigger and then have an assistant hold the light near the infant. If you are using this method, it is important to keep the flash about the same distance from the baby for each image otherwise the photos will be over and under exposed. Again, the important distance is from light to subject, not from camera to subject. Once the lighting distance is correctly determined, the photographer is free to move about the area and still have properly exposed images.

The baby will be able to sit erect without assistance so furniture props could be used. The infant will also be able to pull themselves up to a standing position which will also afford numerous opportunities for great images. The child likes to bounce to music so you could ask the mother what is the favorite type of music is and make sure you have some samples. The baby will follow and grab at bubbles which will provide great pictures that will warm a mother's heart. You could get a bubble machine or simply use a hand devise to make the bubbles. The child will like to play pat-a-cake and peekaboo. This would be a great opportunity to involve mom, dad, or the siblings and get some great family images. They like to roll balls and play with age appropriate toys.

Twelve-month session

As the first birthday approaches the baby will be able to stand and may even be able to walk a short distance with assistance. They will be able to crawl very well and very fast. On their own, they can go from crawling to sitting and climb on furniture. You are probably not going to hold the infant's attention for more than 10 – 15 minutes. It would be best to plan how you are going to provide artificial light, or decide if you are going to use natural light for your images. This would be a good time to experiment with the sun coming through a window as well as various lighting patterns such as split lighting where half of the face is illuminated and the other half is not – the result can be very dramatic.

The baby may be able to use tools such as brushes and combs or a toothbrush. If so this could be used for a picture with mom or dad or the siblings. You will have to be prepared for the shot when it comes because you are probably not going to be successful trying to pose your subject. The child will wave bye-bye which affords many creative ideas. They like to play with containers, filling them with sand and then emptying them. The baby likes to “pick pocket” dad’s shirt. They will flirt with themselves in the mirror. They will be able to stack 2 or 3 large blocks and will like to play with pots and pans, matching lids to pots.

Think about the other things that the infant likes to do for fun. You will most probably have witnessed something that you thought was cute.

Part II: The digital Camera

This section is written for those of you who have, and at least occasionally use, a digital camera but have not felt comfortable in any mode other than automatic. Without going into great detail, Photo Bomb will help you understand what you would be able to accomplish if you were to choose to take control of your camera. For the purpose of this discussion, the assumption is made that you have interchangeable lenses and the ability to shoot in RAW in addition to shooting in .jpg. Do not be concerned if I just lost you. I will explain these terms and what they mean to you. If you're ready to get started, let's go.

Chapter 11
Exposure

There are three settings on your camera which will impact the exposure, meaning how bright or dark the image is. If you change any one of the three settings you will impact the exposure. To be properly exposed the three settings must be balanced. The three settings are f/stop or aperture, shutter speed, and ISO. Think of these as three legs of a triangle.

The f/stop or aperture is the size of the opening in the lens. The larger the opening the more light will be able to reach the sensor in any given time period. This is where it gets confusing because it is counterintuitive, the higher the f/stop the smaller the opening. The aperture is also used to describe how "fast" a lens is. The larger the maximum opening (the smaller the minimum f/stop number) the faster the lens is. The term came about because with a large opening less light was needed to properly expose the film which resulted in a shorter shutter speed and thus the term faster. Typical f/stops will range from f/1.4 (very fast) to f/22.

Next is the shutter speed. This is simply how long the lens is open allowing light to pass through to the sensor. The longer the shutter is open, the more light is allowed to pass through. The shortest time that the lens could be open depends on the camera model, but could be as fast as 1/8000 sec.

Adjustments in shutter speed will also allow you to control the image. If you are taking pictures of a bicycle race you would need to use a fast shutter speed in order to get the fast moving riders sharp in the image. If you are using a slow shutter speed to take pictures of your family in a dark room without the benefit of a tripod, your subjects are probably going to be blurred because of camera shake. Unless you have nerves of steel, you are probably not going to be able to take a sharp image much slower than 1/60 sec. As a rule of thumb, you should be able to hand hold a camera and get a sharp image with a shutter speed of one over the focal length of the lens. To explain, if you were using a 200mm lens instead of the 50mm lens in our example, you would want to select a shutter speed of 1/200 sec. or faster. Since the first available shutter speed on the camera which is at least 1/200 sec is 1/250 sec. you would select that. The quality lenses which are manufactured today generally have a vibration control built into them which would allow you to use slower shutter speeds so that if you had a steady hand, you should be able to take sharp images down to 1/60 sec with the 200 mm lens.

There are times when you would want to use a slower shutter speed for a creative effect. You have probably seen the photograph with the bicycle racer in sharp focus while the background is streaking past out of focus. This effect is created by panning. Panning means that you select a slower shutter speed like 1/30 sec and move the camera to follow the subject as you are taking the picture. This is best done on a tripod so that the camera is only moving in one plane. A word of caution, it might take a lot of practice to get the effect you're looking to achieve.

You have determined the aperture and shutter speed that you need for the creative effect you wish to achieve. The third leg of the triangle of exposure is ISO. This is the sensitivity of the film to light. In a digital camera that is the sensor. The higher the ISO the more sensitive the sensor is to light, meaning the less light it takes to properly expose the image. The ISO is used to get the correct exposure by adjusting the sensitivity of the sensor. In reality, you will probably only adjust the ISO when there is insufficient available light to properly expose the image you want and you don't want to, or can't, use supplemental light like a flash or an additional flash. Generally, you want to have the ISO as low a number as possible. For most cameras that would be either 100 or 200. The ISO will probably go as high as 3200 or even higher depending on your camera.

Why do you need three different setting just to get the exposure right? By adjusting these settings you can begin to control what your image looks like. Let's start with the aperture. Depth of field was discussed earlier. As a reminder, that is the distance between the closest object in the image that is acceptably sharp to the farthest object that is acceptably sharp. You will recall that the distance from the camera impacts the depth of field. The aperture also impacts the depth of field, the higher the aperture (the smaller the opening), the greater the depth of field. In our previous discussion we talked about the iPhone 6 with a depth of field of about 3 inches when photographing an object 10 feet away and a depth of field of about 12 inches when photographing an object 20 feet away. The iPhone has a fixed focal length, it cannot be adjusted. In contrast using an adjustable lens we can significantly increase our ability to get creative. If we assume that the lens on your camera is a 50mm lens set at f/1.4 then those numbers change to 1 ½ inches at 10 feet and 6 inches at 20 feet. However, if the same lens were set to f/16 the depth of field would be 1 ½ feet at a 10 foot distance and

6 1/3 feet at a 20 foot distance. So you could take a photograph of a group with three rows of people and have everyone in focus. You could take a picture of a flower and have everything except for the flower out of focus. You control what is sharp in your image.

Now that you know what the three settings are and how to use them, you need to know what the numbers mean and how to balance them. At any given environmental situation, there are multiple combinations of aperture, shutter speed, and ISO to achieve a proper exposure. In photography all adjustments are referred to as an f/stop change. To change the aperture from f/2.8 to f/4 is one f/stop or simply one stop. That means that the amount of light that can pass through the opening in a set time has been cut in half. To change the aperture to f/5.6 would cut the light in half again. The full f/stop numbers that you would normally use would be f/1.4, f/2, f/2.8, f/4, f/5.6, f/8, f/11, f/16, f/22. Remember that for each full stop the light is cut in half. This means that at f/22 there is only 1/256 the amount of light coming through the lens as would be at f/1.4.

Shutter speeds can vary from a bulb setting where the shutter stays open until you close it to 1/8000 sec. The bulb setting allows for very long exposures such as ten minutes or more if you are, for example, photographing stars. Depending on your camera, the settings would begin at eight sec, then four sec, then two sec, then one sec, then ½, ¼, 1/8, 1/15, 1/30, 1/60, 1/125, 1/250, 1/500, 1/1000, 1/2000, 1/4000, 1/8000. Each of these increments is a full f/stop. As is the case for aperture, each full stop means that the amount of light passing through the lens to the sensor is cut in half.

The ISO numbers generally start at 100 and double for each full f/stop. So at ISO 200 the sensor would be twice as sensitive to light as it was at ISO 100. Most digital cameras would have ISO settings up to 3200. However, professional cameras can be sensitive enough to reach ISO numbers of 256,000. There is a tradeoff for selecting a higher ISO. The higher the number, the more grain you will see in your image. Grain is best described as a texture on the image much like a close up photograph of sand on the beach. The higher the ISO the more obvious the grain becomes. It can get to the point that the image is unusable because it is almost blurred. As a general rule you should be able to go to 1600 ISO without seeing any perceptible grain in your photograph. Modern cameras generally take an acceptable image up to 6400 ISO but you will see the grain at this level.

So now let's put it all together. Any exposure is a combination of these three settings. If I change the aperture by reducing one stop then I need to increase either the shutter speed or the ISO one stop to balance the exposure again. I could also increase both the shutter speed and the ISO by half a stop and achieve the same effect. Most probably this is a little overwhelming. If you want to have full command over the exposure elements of your images using full manual mode you would need to know and understand these concepts.

There is an alternative where you have the ability to control two of the settings and let the camera select the other one. You set the ISO at the lowest possible number, usually 100. Then, there are two choices. You can control the shutter speed and let the camera control the aperture, or you can control the aperture and let the camera control the shutter speed. You can also select auto ISO as a setting in your camera which would allow the camera to control two of the three aspects and you would control only one.

You may choose to use "shutter priority," where you set the shutter speed, for some of your photography, and "aperture priority," where you set the aperture, for others, and "automatic" for most of your images. The difference between these three modes and manual mode is the amount of control that you, the photographer, have over the creation of the image. If you are taking landscape images where you want to get as much of the picture in focus as possible, it would be best to select "aperture priority." You would then want to set your aperture as high as possible (f/16 or f/11). This would give you the greatest depth of field. If you were taking an image of a larger group of people you might want to do the same for the same reason. If you wanted to take a picture of a flower a better solution would be to again use "aperture priority," but this time select a very low aperture number (f/2.8 or f/4) With this setting you would have a very narrow depth of field so that you could isolate the flower by having the foreground and background out of focus.

If you are taking pictures of events which have a lot of random movements, such as your children playing, you might want to select "shutter priority" and a very fast shutter speed (1/500 or 1/1000). This would allow you to freeze the movement of your children and keep the image sharp with no movement from either the camera or the subject. Keep in mind the rule of thumb concerning "longer" lenses. In order to safely hand hold the camera and not have camera shake evident in the image, you want a shutter speed at least equal to one over the focal length of the lens. So you would want to select a shutter speed of 1/250 or faster if using a 200mm lens. This would be another reason to use “shutter priority.” If you were panning with your child as they run past you, you would want to set the shutter speed at 1/30 or 1/15. You would then keep the camera focused on the subject as it moves and press the shutter release. In this case you do not want to stop the camera before you take the picture. Just let it continue to focus on your subject. It is easier said than done, so I would recommend practicing often to hone your skills if you like this effect.

Chapter 12
White Balance

White balance, or color balance, is probably the least understood aspect of photography, yet it is one of the most important if you want your images to reflect what you saw when you took the picture. In its simplest description, white balance is the temperature of the light illuminating the scene. Temperature is not something that we readily associate with color, however, it is the temperature of the light that gives it color. The yellow light coming from an incandescent light bulb is much cooler than the blue sky at midday. You can set the white balance on your camera to auto and let the camera select the best choice. If fact, if you are using your cell phone as your camera you do not have a choice, it is set for automatic selection of white balance. At the other end of the spectrum you could purchase a color light meter and measure the temperature of the light illuminating the scene and enter that temperature (using the Kelvin scale) into your camera for super accurate color rendition. This method is usually limited to professional movie makers. A simpler method would be to set the white balance using the icons on your camera. Refer to your camera manual to see the various icons and what they mean. Basically, you should have icons for daylight, flash, cloudy day, florescent light, tungsten light, incandescent light, and shade. Using these icons to select the white balance will get close in most cases.

There are two settings for white balance which are not intuitive, but they enable getting a more exact measurement. The first is “K” which stands for Kelvin and is used to set an exact light temperature in your camera, the second is “Pre” which stands for preset. You should be able to preset four different white balance values in your camera. Because different cameras have varying methods to achieve the same setting, you should refer to your camera manual to get the procedure for your camera.

If you wish to use “K,” here are some numbers you may find helpful. The blue sky without direct sun is 11,000 degrees Kelvin. A studio strobe is 6,000 degrees. Normal daylight not at sunrise or sunset is 5,000 degrees. A flash bulb (if you still have one) is 4,000 degrees. A normal flood light is 3,200 degrees. A household light bulb is 2,800 degrees. A candle is 1,900 degrees. Today it is possible to purchase daylight bulbs for most lamps which will produce light at 5,500 degrees. Using such bulbs will eliminate the yellow glow that you get when you photograph someone in a room illuminated by light bulbs with a cooler temperature.

If you wish to use “Pre,” remember this stands for preset and is used by the camera to determine, and select, the color temperature of the light falling on the subject. There are two ways to get this value. The first and simplest method is to substitute a piece of white or neutral grey paper for your subject with the same light that you will use for the photograph. Check your camera manual for the exact procedures for using “Pre” on your camera. Generally, to set your white balance to “Pre,” press the WB button and “Pre” should begin to flash. With the sheet of white or grey paper filling the image area press the shutter. There will be a given amount of time, approximately ten seconds, within which you need to press the shutter before the “Pre” stops flashing. You can repeat the process to get the “Pre” to flash again if you need to. You should see “Good” replace “Pre” if you have captured the white balance correctly, if not you should see “No Gd” or “No Good.”

If it is not possible, or is impractical to place the sheet of paper, there is a devise which looks like a filter to fit on your lens called an Expodisc™. You can use an Expodisc™ to capture the white balance. You can get one at your local camera store or online. If you chose to buy an Expodisc™ , you should get a size which is equal to your largest lens. It is possible to hold the disc over a smaller lens, but it must completely cover the lens. To use the devise you would again select "Pre" for the white balance. Then determine the correct exposure if you are setting the shutter speed and aperture manually, or you can select aperture priority and select an aperture setting which will give a correct exposure in the environment surrounding your subject. This time when you press the shutter button you want the camera to be pointing at the light source, not the subject. If you are outdoors, that would be the sky, more specifically, the portion of the sky that your subject was facing. If you were indoors using a lamp or overhead lights you would point the camera at those lights. Again press the WB button and "Pre" will begin to flash. Place the Expodisc™ over your lens and press the shutter button. You should see "Good" or "NoGd." One last thing to keep in mind, with the Expodisc™ it does matter which side of the filter is facing the camera. If you are using the same size filter as your lens opening the Expodisc™ will slip onto the lens just like a filter, but there are no threads. If you are holding the Expodisc™ over your lens because it is larger than the lens opening make sure that the orientation of the filter is the same as it would be for the larger lens.

Whether or not you use automatic white balance, a preset icon, set Kelvin temperature, or use the Expodisc™ will be a matter of personal choice and how important it is to you to get the color of the image accurate. If you are using the post production software program from Adobe® called Lightroom® there is one additional way to get accurate white balance. There is a device from X-Rite™ called the Color Checker Passport™. With this device, you take a picture of the color panel in the same light as your subject. You want the color panel to fill at least half of the image area. It is not critical that the Color Checker Passport™ be in focus, it is important that the light falling on the device be the same as the light falling on your subject. You would then take your images as you normally would, but when you load them into Lightroom® you would select the color eyedropper and click on the white square of the image of the Color Checker Passport™ and Lightroom® will color correct that image. You would then select the remaining images which were taken in the same light and sync the color balance. All of the images will now have the correct white balance. Anytime you change the light which is illuminating the scene/subject you need to repeat this process.

Chapter 13
Supplemental Lighting

Do not be intimidated by the thought of adding your own lighting to the scene you are about to photograph. You will recall from our discussion earlier that the smaller a light source is relative to your subject the harder the light. A hard light means that you have a very distinct shadow and the line between light and shadow is sharp. This is not very flattering for your subject and unless you are trying to take a high contrast image, hard light should be avoided.

Built in Flash and On Camera Flash

You have probably used the built in flash that is part of your camera or cell phone. This is very convenient – it's always with you – and it provides enough light to enable taking the photograph and getting an acceptable image in a fairly dark setting. The built in flash is a very small light. It is not designed to provide soft, flattering light for your subject. It creates hot spots on your subject's forehead and cheeks. If your subject is looking at the camera it will cause the subject's eyes to be red. The intensity of the light also falls off very quickly so that someone standing behind your subject could be underexposed. The one time that the built in flash can provide acceptable results is when you are taking a picture of someone and there is a bright light behind them. This could be the sun or a bright lamp. If you use the built in flash to illuminate your subject, you will now be able to see detail in the subject's face rather than having a silhouette. This effect is known as fill in flash.

You can gain additional control of the light which is illuminating the scene by using a separate flash unit mounted on the camera, an on camera flash. The size of the light source is larger than the built in flash so that the light is softened somewhat. The on camera flash comes in many forms with different capabilities and significantly different costs. The most sophisticated units are able to measure the light put out by the flash, compare it against the amount of light required to correctly expose the scene and turn off the flash when there is enough light. These units, known as "Through The Lens" (TTL) flashes, are able to automatically set the proper flash duration and intensity based upon the camera, the lens, the distance the subject is from the camera, the ISO, the aperture set and the ambient light. The duration of the flash is very short – less than 1/1000 sec to 1/50000 sec. Because of the short duration of the flash, the shutter speed does not affect the exposure of the image. Normally, you would select a shutter speed of 1/60 or 1/125 sec. The TTL flashes are specific to the camera manufacturer. A Nikon flash will not work on a Cannon camera. These flashes have the ability to turn the flash head up and down as well as left and right. You can use this feature to bounce the flash off of the ceiling or a wall to get softer, more pleasant lighting of your subject. The TTL flash will automatically compensate for the increased distance the light must travel when it is bounced off the ceiling or wall and you will still get a properly exposed image.

Manual flash units are significantly less expensive, but you need to determine the flash power or light intensity and the duration of the flash. This is where an understanding of f/stops becomes more important. When using a manual flash, you control the f/stop with the aperture of the lens and the flash power of the flash itself. We have discussed how the aperture impacts the f/stop. If you change from f/4 to f/5.6 that is one f/stop. The amount of light available at the sensor is cut in half. In order to compensate for that loss of light, you need to increase the intensity of the light to double what it was. This can be accomplished on the flash by changing from ¼ power to ½ power. There are adjustments which go from one (full power) to 1/64 or possibly 1/128 power. Each increment is one f/stop. The lower the flash power setting, the shorter the flash duration is. At full power, the flash duration is at its maximum. There is one other adjustment that you can make with the flash. You can change the distance the flash is from the subject. You will recall that if you cut the distance in half, you will double the intensity of the light at the subject. Conversely, it you double the distance, your will cut the intensity in half.

Most manual flashes will allow you to move the flash head up and down and left and right. Here is where is gets complicated. Remember the light intensity at the subject is cut in half if you double the distance from the flash to the subject. If you are standing ten feet away from your subject and you turn the flash head to bounce off the white wall which is five feet to your right, you have just increased the distance the light is traveling to get to the subject. By applying trigonometry to the situation, you could compute the exact increase in the distance and thereby determine the adjustment that you would need to make to the aperture or the flash power setting. Most photographers are not able to compute that in their head in the instant that they have to take the picture. They do, however, know that they need to increase the flash power if they are bouncing the flash. If they forget to compensate for the increased flash to subject distance, they know why the image was suddenly underexposed.

Off camera flash

You begin to get total control of the lighting of your subject when you use an off camera flash. That means that the flash is located at a point that will afford the best lighting. The flash must then communicate with the camera to know when to fire to coincide with the opening of camera's shutter. Originally, this communication was accomplished with a long cord connecting the two. As you might imagine this could lead to people stumbling over the cord or pulling over the flash if they ran into the cord. The latest technology uses radio waves to communicate between the two devices. This allows the flash to be triggered up to 300 feet away from the camera and even behind buildings or cars or other obstacles. Multiple frequencies are available so that several flashes can be used in the same area without interfering with each other. This allows the photographer to set up flashes that will be used for a wide angle image showing the whole room which are different from the flashes which would be used for close up pictures with fewer people, such as the bride and groom during their first dance as husband and wife. When working with off camera flashes the most important thing to remember is that it is the distance from the flash to the subject that determines the exposure. The camera can be anywhere. You can move while you are taking pictures to get different views and perspectives. The subject will always be correctly exposed. If you are using TTL technology to trigger the flash units, the camera will automatically turn off the flash as soon as enough light has been detected. If you are using a manual flash you will need to calculate the flash power and aperture appropriate for the distance from the flash to the subject as discussed above. You can use multiple off camera flashes to provide light on both sides of the subject. You can use another to create a highlight in the hair and yet another to create a ribbon of light across the subject's shoulder to provide separation from the background. You are limited only by your imagination and the number of flashes and remote triggers you have to work with. Each flash will need its own trigger and there needs to be a transmitter on the camera to send the signal to the triggers.

Studio strobes

Studio strobes are a larger, more powerful source of artificial light. They are powered by household electrical systems, but there are portable batteries which have sufficient power to use the strobes in the outdoor environment. These strobes are much heavier and bulkier than flash units. They are normally mounted on light stands simply because it is too difficult to hand hold them. The advantage that they have over flash units is the amount of light and the speed with which multiple sequential images can be properly exposed. The light produced by these strobes is beautiful. A light modifier, which will be discussed in the next section, is normally attached making the relative size of the light source even larger which gives the light a nice soft wrap-around quality. In the studio the photographer uses multiple strobes to sculpt the light around the subject getting effects that are extremely difficult to achieve with flash units. Using the light to bring out the desired highlights and using a less intense light to emphasize the shadows the photographer creates the professional portrait. Contrary to what most people think, it is the shadows that give an object dimension. The shadows create the three dimensional illusion on a two dimensional sheet of paper. Many very successful professional photographers use studio strobes for all of their images because of the quality of the light produced. Even when working in the field they will have enough assistants to move the multiple lights from scene to scene.

Light modifiers

A light modifier does just that, it modifies the light being produced by the light source. This could be as simple as blocking the sun at mid-day with a board or the wall of a building thereby getting the subject into an environment with less contrast and softer light. As a light blocker or GOBO (Go Between) the light modifier could be opaque, totally blocking the light, or it could be translucent merely blocking the harshness of the light while allowing the light to continue to illuminate the scene. By using a translucent material, you are essentially creating a light box for the light source. A light box is placed around the light source such as a studio strobe or a flash unit. The sides are opaque while the surface facing the subject is translucent. Some light boxes have a second translucent face so that the light is softened and then softened again before it gets to the subject. The advantage of using a second translucent face is that the light gets very soft and wraparound. The disadvantage is that you lose light intensity every time it goes through another modifier. You will lose one to two stops by using a light modifier. Light boxes come in various shapes and sizes. The largest are octaboxes, octagonal or eight sided. They can be as large as six feet across. There are square boxes which are generally quite large three to five feet on a side. There are rectangular light boxes which are very popular for producing a separation light on the shoulder or a hair light to provide distinction from the background. Rectangular light boxes are typically one foot wide and three or four feet long. The light boxes can be further modified by a device known as the egg crate grid. This is a black cloth cover for the light box which has square openings and is about one inch thick. It looks like the packing material used to protect eggs, hence the name. The purpose of the egg crate is to focus the light and to prevent it from falling on the background or the other side of the subject. For example, you might want to have a dark background. The egg crate grid would prevent the light from the modifier which was providing light for your subject from falling on the background and making it lighter. The large octaboxes and square light boxes are used as the main light source, called a key light. Because we read the written sentence from left to right, you would normally place the main light on the subject's right, your left. A slightly smaller and less intense light modifier would be placed on the other side as a fill light. This makes the left side of the image brighter than the right side which feels natural to the viewer.

Other light modifiers would include an umbrella. The umbrella can be used to reflect the light back past the light source or it can be used as a shoot-through umbrella in which case, as you may suspect, the umbrella is between the light source and the subject. If you are using the umbrella to reflect the light back past the light source to the subject you are losing some of the intensity of the light through the umbrella. To reduce this loss, an opaque cover can be placed over the umbrella. The effect of the umbrella is similar to that of the light box.

The next light modifier would be the reflector. Reflectors come in various sizes and shapes from four by six feet in a frame to a few inches in a collapsible reflector. The most popular are the multiple cover three-foot collapsible circular reflectors. They would have white, black, silver, gold, and zebra faces. Just to refresh your memory, the white face would give a soft, but weak reflection. This is good for working in the bright sun at mid-day. The black face would be used to subtract light either as a GOBO or to reduce reflections, called specular highlights, in people's forehead or on metal objects such as a silver tea service. The silver face reflects a lot of light. It would be used when the sun was not so intense or when working with indoor lighting. The gold face also reflects a lot of light, but it also warms the light. This effect is often used to make people look more alive. It provides a mini-tan. The zebra face has the same effect as the gold or silver face, but it is less intense. The zebra face has alternating white and either gold or silver stripes.

Chapter 14
Other Things To Consider

RAW vs .jpg

Photo Bomb includes a discussion on the debate as to whether it is better to take your pictures in .jpg format or to record them as RAW images. This discussion provides the information so that you are aware that there is a difference and makes you aware what that difference means. The RAW format is available on most digital cameras and there is even an app available which will allow you to capture RAW images with an iPhone. Simply stated, with the RAW format all of the information that is captured at the time the image is taken is saved to the image file. There is no processing in the camera and you have the maximum ability to modify the image using post processing software. When you save your images in the .jpg format the camera actually processes the file data, makes some decisions about the white balance, color rendering, and exposure and compresses the file to make it much smaller. Regardless which format you have chosen, the image that is shown on the LED on the camera is in .jpg format. This is why the image you see on the back of your camera may appear different when you look at the actual RAW file. Which is better? That really depends on how much post processing you want to do. For the majority of photographers the .jpg is the correct choice. Most professional photographers use the RAW format merely because it gives them the most control over what their image looks like and they are able to make the decisions about white balance and even adjust it if the memory of the scene is different from what the computer is showing them. The major disadvantage of saving an image as a .jpg file is that every time you save the image, you lose a little bit of quality. If you make many minor changes to how you cropped the image, or the exposure, etc. the quality may deteriorate so badly that you may not be able to even use the image. Unless you saved a copy of the original file, you cannot go back and start over. The lesson here is if you save your images in .jpg format, make a copy of the original file before you start to make corrections.

Software

There are numerous software programs which can organize and process your photographs. This discussion will center around the more advanced programs because that is what

I use. The simplest and least expensive program used by most professional photographers is Lightroom® by Adobe®. You can organize your photographs by date the image was captured, by date the image was last processed, by camera that was used to make the image, by keywords, by your determination of the quality of the image, or any other method you can imagine. Through judicious use of keywords you could immediately identify and display every photograph you had ever taken of "little Gabby." You could then export all of those images to a file on a thumb drive or to an album that you were creating. The amount of processing that you would be able to achieve on the individual images would depend on whether or not you were saving your images in your camera as RAW or .jpg files. If you chose to use .jpg, which most photographers do, you would still be able to make minor adjustments to the white balance, adjust the exposure, and modify the individual areas of the photograph such as the highlights and shadows. For most photographers, this program will enable you to complete all of the processing that you would want or need to do. However, if you want to have total control over the software manipulated resulting image, you should consider changing your format to RAW. As the artist you have complete control of the final product. The disadvantage is that you need to understand each of the items that go into the image in order to correct them. You need to learn how to apply the software program. So the bottom line is that it requires more commitment on your part to learn how to best use the tools available.

The next program that most professional photographers use is probably the most well known, Adobe® Photoshop®. This is a very powerful image processing software program. With it your ability to create an image is limited only by your ability to imagine what could be. However, if you are new to the program, be prepared for a learning curve. Most people learn how to do the few things that they like to do for every image and then get more proficient at those skills without ever feeling a need to expand to the innumerable additional capabilities. The more experience you have using the program the more additional capabilities will be added to your skill set.

If you want to create images that totally blow your friends away, you will need to learn how to post process your photographs. The reality today is that no matter how well you correct the image in your camera before you take the picture, you will want/need to modify the image to get it to "pop."

This list is by no means thorough. There are many other software programs which perform the same functions as the ones described here. Your decision to use any software program should be based on your needs and the output of the product you are using. Nearly all software programs provide an evaluation version of the application. Take advantage of the opportunity to use the software and properly evaluate whether or not it is right for your needs.

Chapter 15
The Value of a Professional Photographer

We rely on professionals every day. We do not question the value that they provide when we get the bill for their goods or services. If your roof has a leak you are going to have it repaired. You are probably not going to select the roofer who provides the lowest quote. Why not? Is it because we know that we get what we pay for and when it comes to our health and comfort we get what we want and pay whatever is asked of us when the bill arrives. The same logic applies when we look for plumbers, electricians, landscapers, or handy men to maintain or repair minor issues in our homes. When we look for an interior designer we look for a style that we like. The price is not a consideration when selecting our designer. If the price is beyond our budget we would normally wait until we had saved enough money to pay for the services rather than selecting another designer who charged less, especially if we didn't like their style.

We are willing to pay for event planners even though we could easily plan the event ourselves. Why is that? Is it because the event planner is an expert in coordinating people and services to achieve that memorable event? Is it because it is so much easier to let the expert do the work and the results are so much better? We pay a mechanic to maintain and repair our cars. Even though we might have mechanical skills, the necessary equipment is complex and expensive. It is cost effective and less challenging to rely on the expertise of the mechanic.

Is there anyone who would recommend being your own doctor or dentist. Can you imagine buying a scalpel from e-Bay so that you could perform an appendectomy on your child in your living room? These examples have gone from the sublime to the ridiculous. The point I am trying to make is that we are comfortable paying for professional services. We are willing to pay for someone who has the education and training to become competent in their field. When we need their services or product it is the value we look at, not the cost. Cost is what you pay, value is what you get. Is there a cost you would not pay to get your children healthy and happy following an accident or illness? As long as you had the means to pay, you would be willing to pay whatever it took.

Now to make the point, professional photographers have invested time and money into themselves to improve their skill sets and into their equipment to enable them to go beyond the snapshot. Having a camera does not make one a photographer, any more than having a stethoscope makes one a doctor. You can use the tool to achieve an end, but what about the education and experience to effectively employ the tool.